MathFlare

Name: ______________________

Class: ___________

Teacher: ______________________

Introduction

As parents and educators, we recognize the pivotal role mathematics plays in shaping a child's academic journey and future success. Yet, the path to mathematical proficiency can often seem daunting, fraught with challenges and complexities. That's where the transformative power of MathFlare Workbooks shine through, illuminating the way forward with clarity, precision, and purpose.

Introducing MathFlare Workbooks – a beacon of guidance, a testament to excellence, and a catalyst for achievement. Crafted with meticulous care and expertise, MathFlare Workbooks stand as paragons of educational excellence, designed to nurture young minds, ignite a passion for learning, and develop a deep-rooted understanding of mathematical concepts.

Picture this: your child eagerly delves into the pages of Mathflare Workbook, greeted by a step-by-step guide illuminated with vivid examples that demystify complex mathematical concepts. With each turn of the page, they embark on a journey of discovery, encountering thoughtfully curated practice questions that reinforce learning and hone problem-solving skills. And when they unveil the answers to those very questions, a sense of accomplishment blossoms within them – a tangible reward for their hard work and dedication.

But MathFlare Workbooks are more than just tools for learning; they are pathways to comprehension, fostering a deep-seated understanding of mathematical concepts through a sequential, logical flow. From fundamental principles to advanced problem-solving strategies, every chapter builds upon the last, ensuring a robust foundation upon which future knowledge can be constructed.

As parents, we yearn for nothing more than to see our children thrive, to witness the spark of inspiration ignited within them as they conquer academic challenges with confidence and poise. MathFlare Workbooks serve as partners in this noble endeavor, offering not just practice questions, but the keys to unlocking a world of opportunity.

And for teachers, MathFlare Workbooks stand as invaluable allies in the quest to cultivate mathematical proficiency in the classroom. With answers readily available, instructors can focus on guiding and nurturing their students, confident in the knowledge that MathFlare Workbooks provide a solid framework upon which to build.

In the pages of MathFlare Workbooks, we find not just the promise of academic excellence, but the seeds of a brighter tomorrow. So let us embrace the power of mathematics, let us champion the journey of learning, and let us pave the way for a generation of young minds poised to shape the world. With MathFlare Workbooks as our guide, the possibilities are infinite, and the future, bright.

Table of Contents

MathFlare
Grade 2
MATH WORKBOOK
Step by Step Guide and Essential Practice with Answers
Addition Subtraction
Multiplication
Place Value and Expanded Notations
Geometry
MathFlare Publishing

MathFlare
Grade 2-3
MATH WORKBOOK
Step by Step Guide and Essential Practice with Answers
Addition Subtraction
Multiplication and Division
Place Value and Expanded Notations
Geometry
MathFlare Publishing

MathFlare
Grade 3
MATH WORKBOOK
Step by Step Guide and Essential Practice with Answers
Multiplication and Division
Decimals
Place Value and Expanded Notations
Fractions and Geometry
MathFlare Publishing

MathFlare
Grade 1
MATH WORKBOOK
Step by Step Guide and Essential Practice with Answers
Counting and Numbers
Addition and Subtraction
Place Value and Expanded Notations
Understanding Time
MathFlare Publishing

MathFlare
Grade 1-2
MATH WORKBOOK
Step by Step Guide and Essential Practice with Answers
Counting and Numbers
Addition and Subtraction
Place Value and Expanded Notations
Understanding Time
MathFlare Publishing

MathFlare
Grade 3-4
MATH WORKBOOK
Step by Step Guide and Essential Practice with Answers
Addition Subtraction
Multiplication Division
Place Value and Expanded Notations
Fractions and Geometry
MathFlare Publishing

MathFlare
Grade 4
MATH WORKBOOK
Step by Step Guide and Essential Practice with Answers
Addition Subtraction
Multiplication Division
Place Value and Expanded Notations
Fractions and Geometry
MathFlare Publishing

MathFlare
Grade 4-5
MATH WORKBOOK
Step by Step Guide and Essential Practice with Answers
Multiplication Division
Place Value and Expanded Notations
Fractions and Geometry
Unit Conversion
MathFlare Publishing

MathFlare
Grade 5
MATH
WORKBOOK
Step by Step Guide
and Essential Practice
with Answers
Multiplication Division
Place Value and Expanded Notations
Fractions and Geometry
Unit Conversion
MathFlare Publishing

MathFlare
Grade 5-6
MATH
WORKBOOK
Step by Step Guide
and Essential Practice
with Answers
Multiplication Division
Place Value and Expanded Notations
Fractions and Geometry
Units and Statistics
MathFlare Publishing

MathFlare
Grade 6
MATH
WORKBOOK
Step by Step Guide
and Essential Practice
with Answers
Integers and Statistics
Arithmetic and Pre-Algebra
Fractions and Geometry
Ratio and Percentage
MathFlare Publishing

MathFlare
Grade 6-7
MATH
WORKBOOK
Step by Step Guide
and Essential Practice
with Answers
Arithmetic and Pre-Algebra
Ratio, Percent Proportion
Geometry
Statistics
MathFlare Publishing

MathFlare
Grade 7
MATH
WORKBOOK
Step by Step Guide
and Essential Practice
with Answers
Pre-Algebra
Ratio, Percent Proportion
Geometry
Statistics
MathFlare Publishing

MathFlare
Grade 7-8
MATH
WORKBOOK
Step by Step Guide
and Essential Practice
with Answers
Pre-Algebra
Ratio, Percent Proportion
Geometry and Cartesian Plane
Statistics
MathFlare Publishing

MathFlare
Grade 8-9
MATH
WORKBOOK
Step by Step Guide
and Essential Practice
with Answers
Pre-Algebra
Ratio, Proportion and Percentage
Linear Equations
Geometry and Cartesian Plane
MathFlare Publishing

MathFlare
Grade 8
MATH
WORKBOOK
Step by Step Guide
and Essential Practice
with Answers
Pre-Algebra
Percentage
Linear Equations
Geometry
MathFlare Publishing

Exponents and Scientific Notations

Exponents

An exponent tells us how many times a number (called the base) is multiplied by itself. It is written as a superscript to the right of the base number. For example, in 2^3, 2 is the base and 3 is the exponent.

Rules:

1. **Product Rule**: When multiplying powers with the same base, add the exponents.

$$a^m \times a^n = a^{m+n}$$

For example:

$$2^3 = 2 \times 2 \times 2 = 8$$

$$3^2 \times 3^4 = 3^{2+4} = 3^6 = 3 \times 3 \times 3 \times 3 \times 3 \times 3 = 729$$

2. **Quotient Rule**: When dividing powers with the same base, subtract the exponents.

$$a^m \div a^n = a^{m-n}$$

For example:

$$5^3 \div 5^2 = 5^{3-2} = 5^1 = 5$$

3. **Power of a Power Rule**: When raising a power to another power, multiply the exponents.

$$(a^m)^n = a^{mn}$$

For example:

$$(2^2)^3 = 2^{2\times3} = 2^6 = 64$$

4. **Power of a Product Rule**: When raising a product to a power, distribute the power to each factor.

$$(ab)^n = a^n \times b^n$$

For example:

$$(2\times3)^2 = 2^2 \times 3^2 = 4 \times 9 = 36$$

5. **Power of a Quotient Rule**: When raising a quotient to a power, distribute the power to the numerator and denominator separately.

$$\left(\frac{a}{b}\right)^n = \frac{a^n}{b^n}$$

For example:

$$\left(\frac{4}{2}\right)^3 = \frac{4^3}{2^3} = \frac{64}{8} = 8$$

6. **Zero Exponent Rule**: Any nonzero number raised to the power of zero equals 11.

$$a^0 = 1$$

For example:

$$7^0 = 1$$

7. **Negative Exponent Rule**: A negative exponent means the reciprocal of the base raised to the positive exponent.

$$a^{-n} = \frac{1}{a^n}$$

For example:

$$2^{-3} = \frac{1}{2^3} = \frac{1}{8}$$

To evaluate expressions with exponents, we can use:

- **Repeated Multiplication**: Perform the multiplication indicated by the exponent.

- **Using the Rules of Exponents**: Apply the appropriate rule to simplify expressions involving exponents.

Scientific Notations

Scientific notation is a way to express very large or very small numbers in a concise and convenient manner. It involves writing a number as the product of a coefficient (a number between 1 and 10) and a power of 10.

This allows us to represent numbers with many zeros or decimal places more efficiently, making them easier to work with in calculations and comparisons.

$$a \times 10^n$$

where a is the coefficient (a number between 1 and 10) and n is the exponent, which indicates the power of 10.

For example:

Let's take the number 45,000 and express it in scientific notation.

To express 45,000 in scientific notation, we need to move the decimal point to the right until there is only one non-zero digit to its left.

1. Count the number of places we moved the decimal point. Since we moved it 4 places to the left, the exponent n will be -4.

2. The coefficient a is the number we obtain after moving the decimal point. In this case, it is 4.5.

3. Therefore, 45,000 in scientific notation is:

$$4.5 \times 10^4$$

To convert 4.5×10^4 back into standard notation, we need to multiply the coefficient 4.5 by 10 raised to the power of 4.

$$4.5 \times 10^4 = 4.5 \times (10 \times 10 \times 10 \times 10)$$

$$= 4.5 \times 10000$$

$$= 45000$$

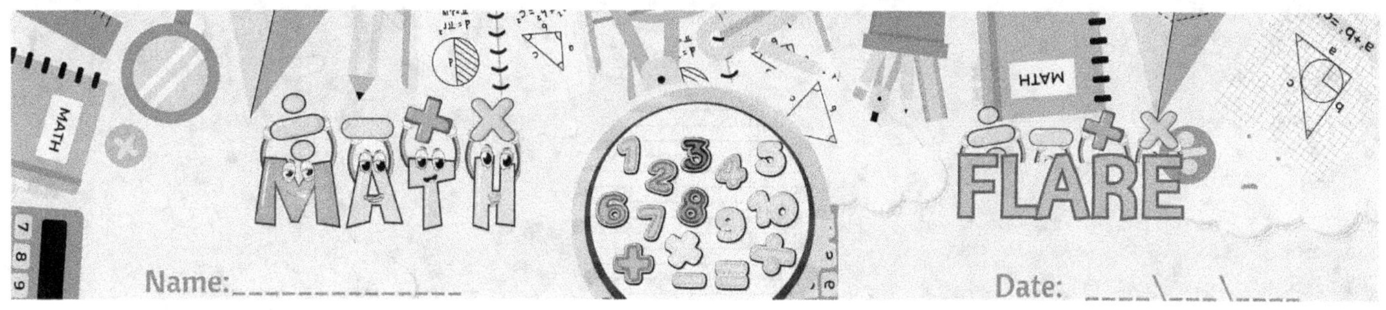

Exponents

Convert the values.

1. $17^4 = $ ______________________

2. $17^5 = $ ______________________

3. $2^3 = $ ______________________

4. $7^4 = $ ______________________

5. $16^{-4} = $ ______________________

6. $8^0 = $ ______________________

7. $11^2 = $ ______________________

8. $15^{-3} = $ ______________________

9. $15^{-2} = $ ______________________

10. $5^5 = $ ______________________

11. $10^1 = $ ______________________

12. $6^{-5} = $ ______________________

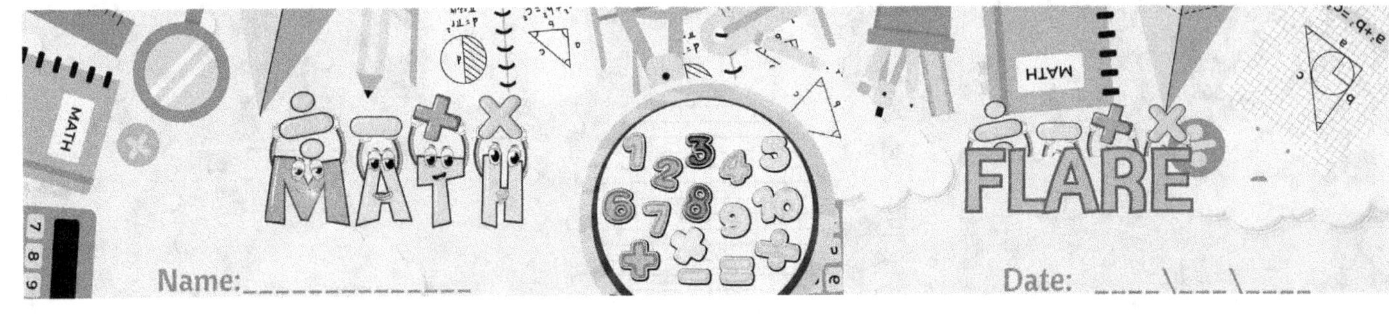

13. $3^3 =$ _______________

14. $13^2 =$ _______________

15. $20^1 =$ _______________

16. $10^2 =$ _______________

17. $10^0 =$ _______________

18. $9^0 =$ _______________

19. $7^{-1} =$ _______________

20. $12^5 =$ _______________

21. $3^{-5} =$ _______________

22. $12^4 =$ _______________

23. $16^5 =$ _______________

24. $4^{-3} =$ _______________

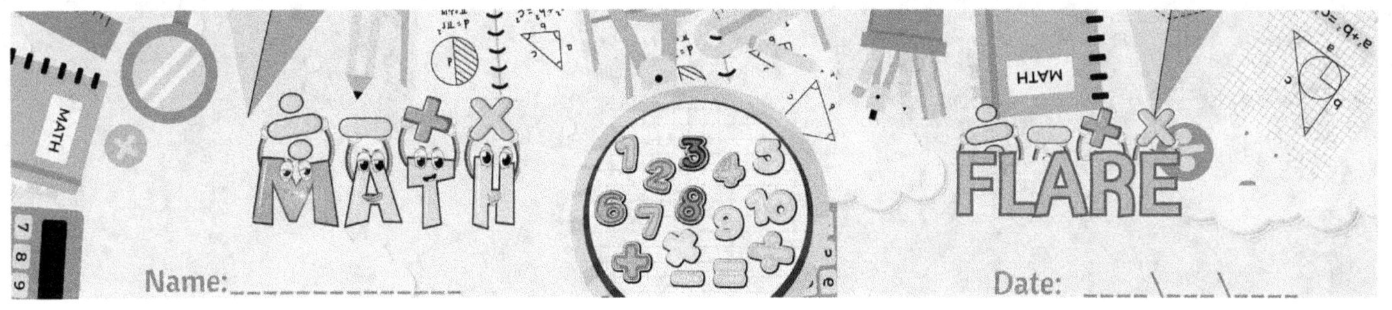

25. $17^3 =$ _______________

26. $17^2 =$ _______________

27. $3^{-1} =$ _______________

28. $16^4 =$ _______________

29. $10^4 =$ _______________

30. $18^{-1} =$ _______________

31. $7^{-5} =$ _______________

32. $6^3 =$ _______________

33. $4^3 =$ _______________

34. $14^{-1} =$ _______________

35. $6^1 =$ _______________

36. $2^{-5} =$ _______________

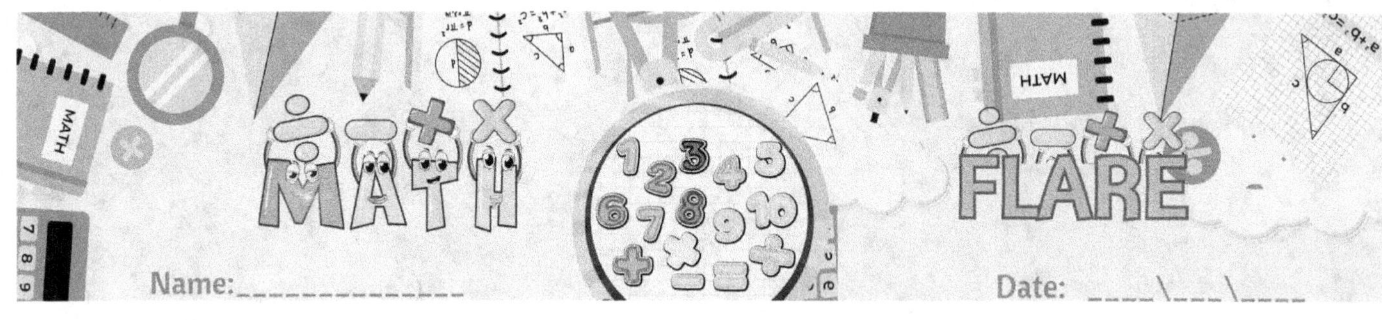

37. $19^{-3} =$ _______________

38. $12^{1} =$ _______________

39. $1^{3} =$ _______________

40. $13^{3} =$ _______________

41. $6^{2} =$ _______________

42. $5^{-1} =$ _______________

43. $12^{-4} =$ _______________

44. $4^{-4} =$ _______________

45. $15^{-4} =$ _______________

46. $18^{-4} =$ _______________

47. $20^{5} =$ _______________

48. $14^{2} =$ _______________

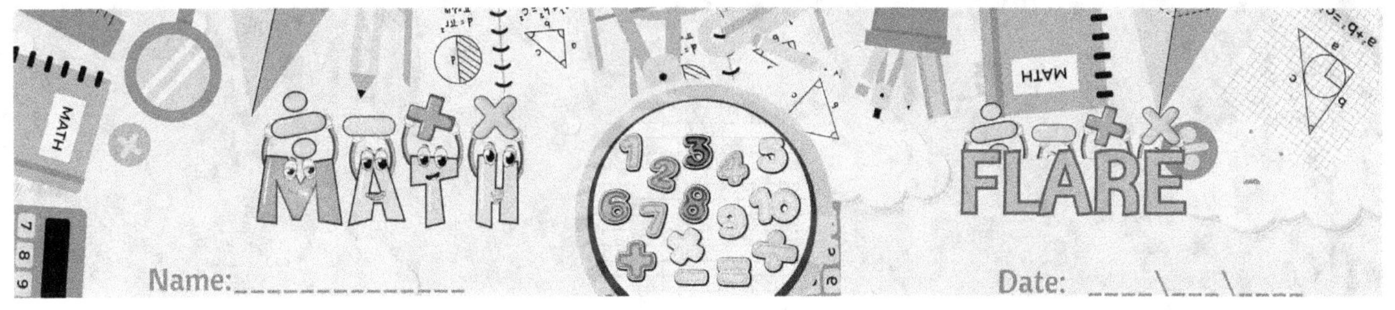

49. $19^{-5} =$ ______________________

50. $6^{-4} =$ ______________________

51. $5^{1} =$ ______________________

52. $6^{-3} =$ ______________________

53. $4^{-1} =$ ______________________

54. $11^{-4} =$ ______________________

55. $10^{-4} =$ ______________________

56. $13^{1} =$ ______________________

57. $20^{2} =$ ______________________

58. $16^{1} =$ ______________________

59. $17^{0} =$ ______________________

60. $4^{1} =$ ______________________

Name:_____________________ Date: ______________

61. $9^1 =$ ________________

62. $10^3 =$ ________________

63. $15^5 =$ ________________

64. $10^{-1} =$ ________________

65. $7^{-4} =$ ________________

66. $4^{-2} =$ ________________

67. $20^{-5} =$ ________________

68. $13^5 =$ ________________

69. $6^{-2} =$ ________________

70. $17^{-5} =$ ________________

71. $15^{-1} =$ ________________

72. $4^4 =$ ________________

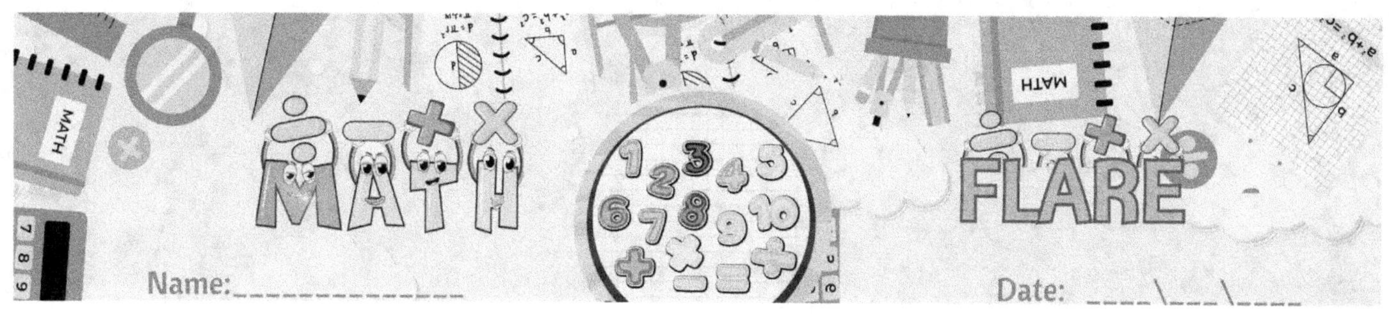

73. $1^4 =$ ________________

74. $7^0 =$ ________________

75. $9^5 =$ ________________

76. $18^3 =$ ________________

77. $11^4 =$ ________________

78. $1^1 =$ ________________

79. $10^5 =$ ________________

80. $5^4 =$ ________________

81. $7^5 =$ ________________

82. $20^4 =$ ________________

83. $14^{-4} =$ ________________

84. $11^0 =$ ________________

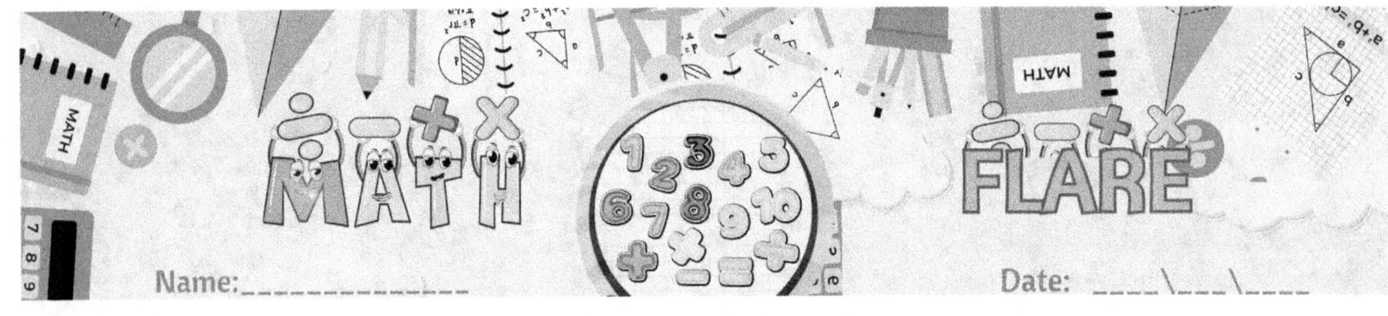

85. $5^2 =$ _______________

86. $8^{-2} =$ _______________

87. $3^1 =$ _______________

88. $4^2 =$ _______________

89. $7^1 =$ _______________

90. $9^2 =$ _______________

91. $14^0 =$ _______________

92. $1^5 =$ _______________

93. $8^{-5} =$ _______________

94. $11^1 =$ _______________

95. $3^5 =$ _______________

96. $18^{-3} =$ _______________

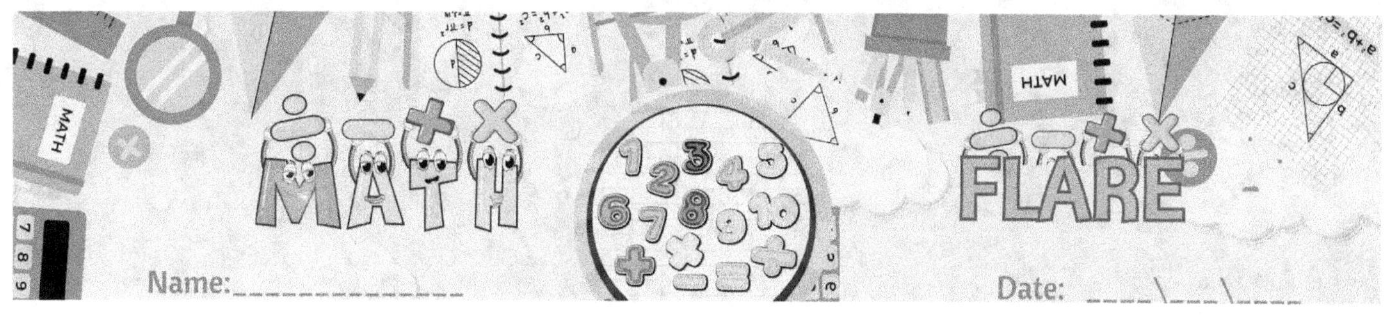

97. 11^3 = _______________

98. 8^{-1} = _______________

99. 18^{-5} = _______________

100. 16^3 = _______________

101. 17^1 = _______________

102. 12^{-3} = _______________

103. 2^2 = _______________

104. 6^{-1} = _______________

105. 20^{-4} = _______________

106. 14^{-5} = _______________

107. 13^{-4} = _______________

108. 18^5 = _______________

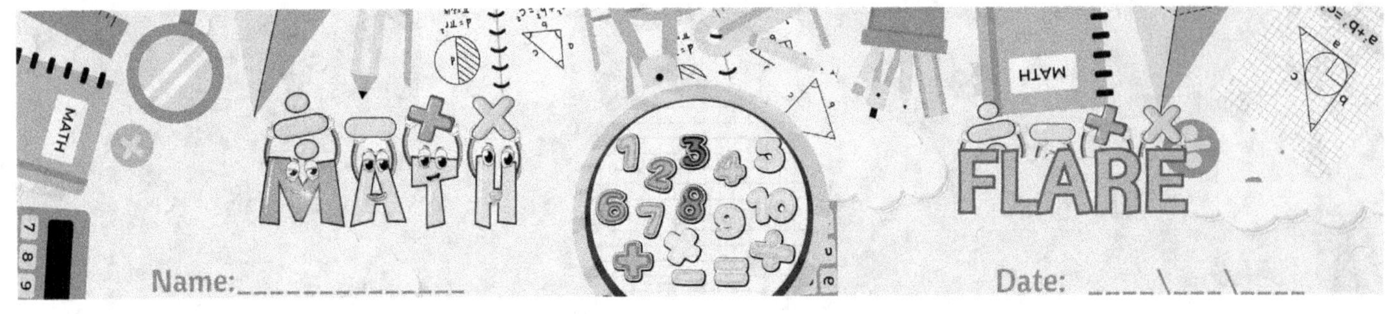

109. 10^{-5} = ______________

110. 15^{3} = ______________

111. 3^{-3} = ______________

112. 2^{-1} = ______________

113. 11^{5} = ______________

114. 1^{-4} = ______________

115. 8^{2} = ______________

116. 18^{0} = ______________

117. 9^{-4} = ______________

118. 20^{-1} = ______________

119. 18^{1} = ______________

120. 20^{-2} = ______________

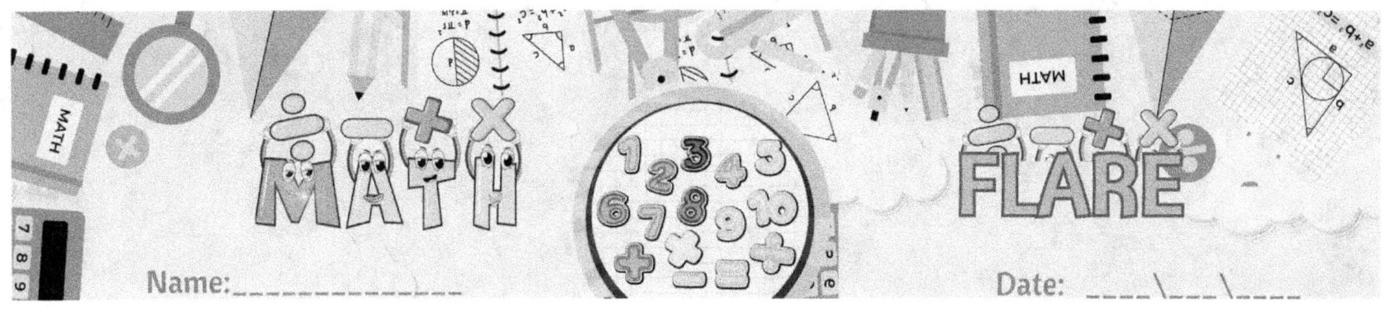

121. $2^{-2} =$ _______________

122. $4^{-5} =$ _______________

123. $17^{-1} =$ _______________

124. $1^{0} =$ _______________

125. $19^{5} =$ _______________

126. $9^{4} =$ _______________

127. $2^{5} =$ _______________

128. $5^{3} =$ _______________

129. $14^{4} =$ _______________

130. $20^{0} =$ _______________

131. $8^{-3} =$ _______________

132. $19^{-2} =$ _______________

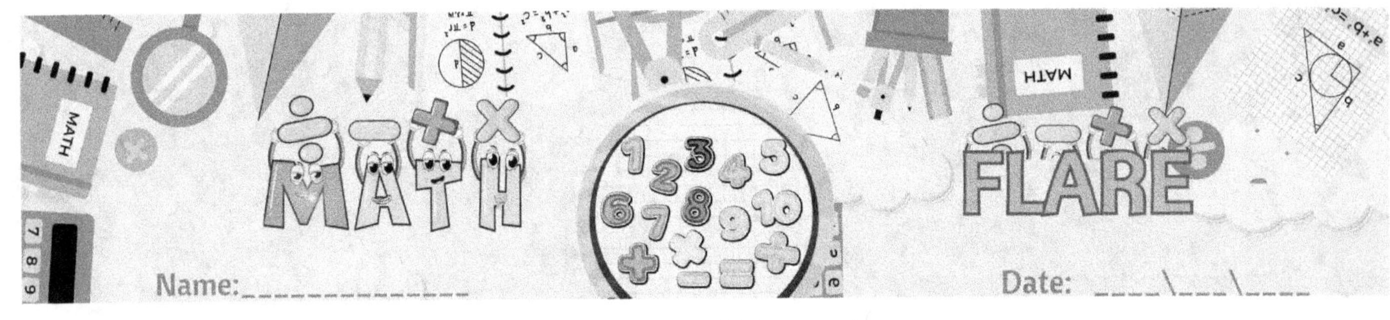

133. $4^0 =$ _______________

134. $11^{-5} =$ _______________

135. $8^5 =$ _______________

136. $3^2 =$ _______________

137. $12^{-1} =$ _______________

138. $3^4 =$ _______________

139. $16^{-1} =$ _______________

140. $13^{-5} =$ _______________

141. $19^3 =$ _______________

142. $1^{-3} =$ _______________

143. $20^3 =$ _______________

144. $17^{-4} =$ _______________

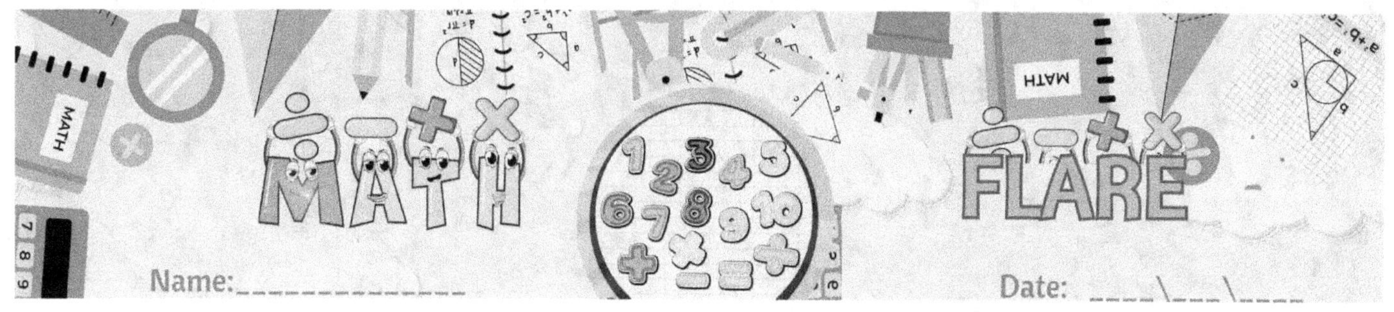

145. 2^{-4} = _______________

146. 16^{-5} = _______________

147. 9^{-5} = _______________

148. 19^{-4} = _______________

149. 17^{-3} = _______________

150. 4^{5} = _______________

151. 3^{-4} = _______________

152. 8^{1} = _______________

153. 15^{1} = _______________

154. 13^{-2} = _______________

155. 6^{5} = _______________

156. 19^{4} = _______________

157. 10^{-2} = _______________

158. 5^{0} = _______________

159. 13^{4} = _______________

160. 2^{0} = _______________

161. 18^{2} = _______________

162. 14^{5} = _______________

163. 3^{0} = _______________

164. 15^{2} = _______________

165. 9^{-3} = _______________

166. 18^{-2} = _______________

167. 14^{1} = _______________

168. 2^{4} = _______________

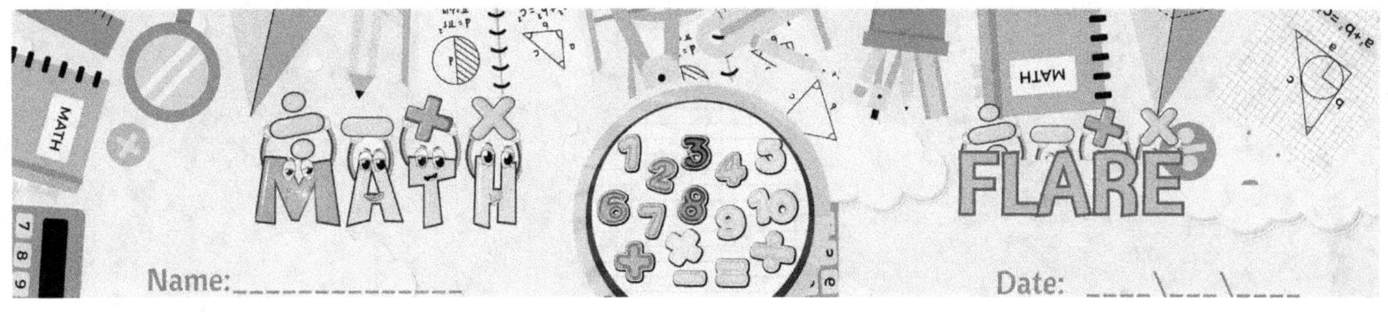

169. $16^{-3} =$ _______________

170. $15^{4} =$ _______________

171. $12^{-5} =$ _______________

172. $9^{-1} =$ _______________

173. $20^{-3} =$ _______________

174. $7^{2} =$ _______________

175. $9^{3} =$ _______________

176. $12^{2} =$ _______________

177. $12^{3} =$ _______________

178. $6^{4} =$ _______________

179. $8^{3} =$ _______________

180. $15^{0} =$ _______________

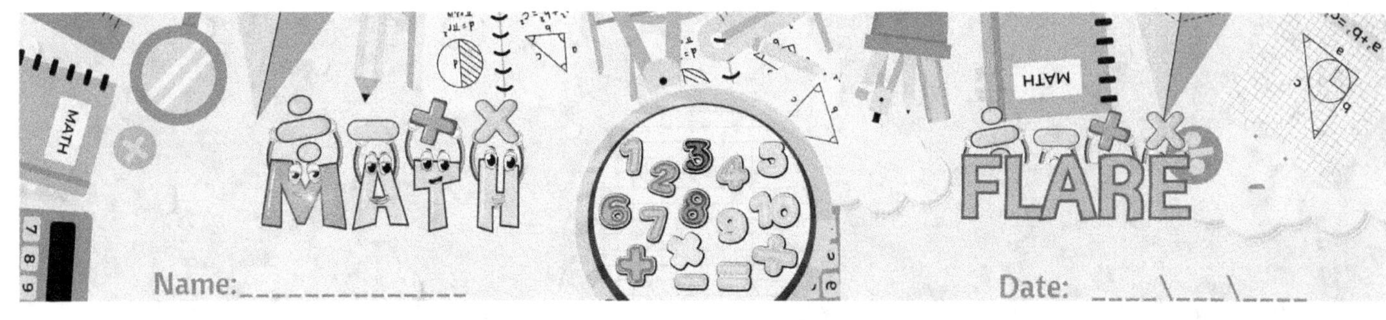

181. $13^{-3} =$ ______________________

182. $1^{-2} =$ ______________________

183. $5^{-5} =$ ______________________

184. $7^{3} =$ ______________________

185. $19^{2} =$ ______________________

186. $18^{4} =$ ______________________

187. $5^{-4} =$ ______________________

188. $1^{2} =$ ______________________

189. $13^{0} =$ ______________________

190. $12^{-2} =$ ______________________

191. $15^{-5} =$ ______________________

192. $8^{4} =$ ______________________

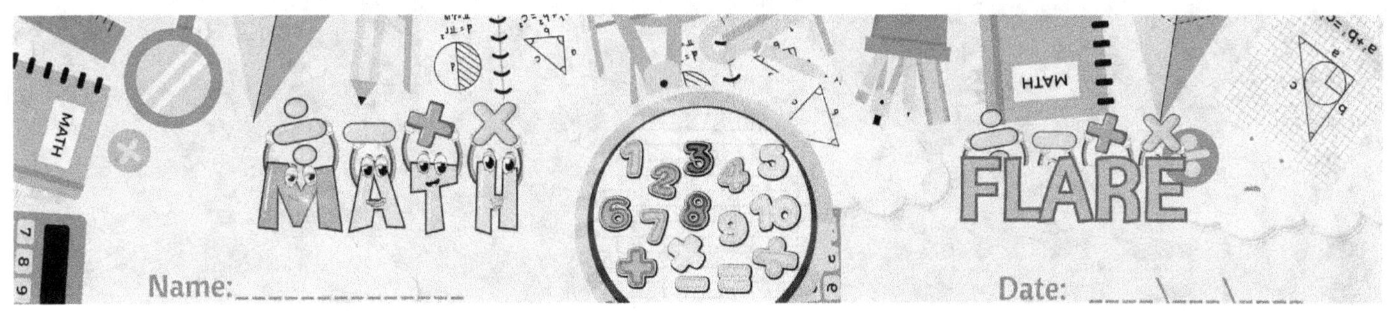

193. 14^{3} =

194. 8^{-4} =

195. 14^{-3} =

196. 9^{-2} =

197. 12^{0} =

198. 7^{-3} =

199. 17^{-2} =

200. 13^{-1} =

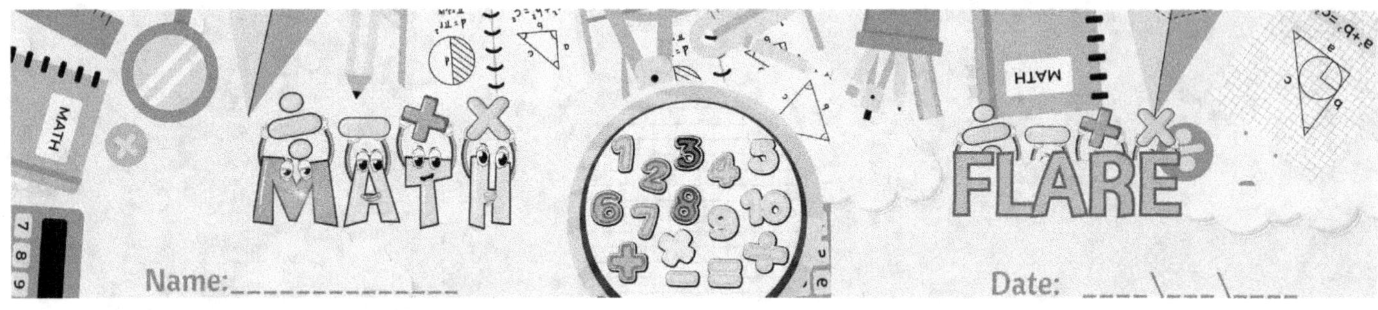

Scientific Notation

Provide the scientific notation for each value.

201. $61,000,000 =$ _______________________________

202. $4.35 \times 10^{7} =$ _______________________________

203. $89,640,000 =$ _______________________________

204. $74,710,000 =$ _______________________________

205. $30,920,000 =$ _______________________________

206. $69,000,000 =$ _______________________________

207. $67,300,000 =$ _______________________________

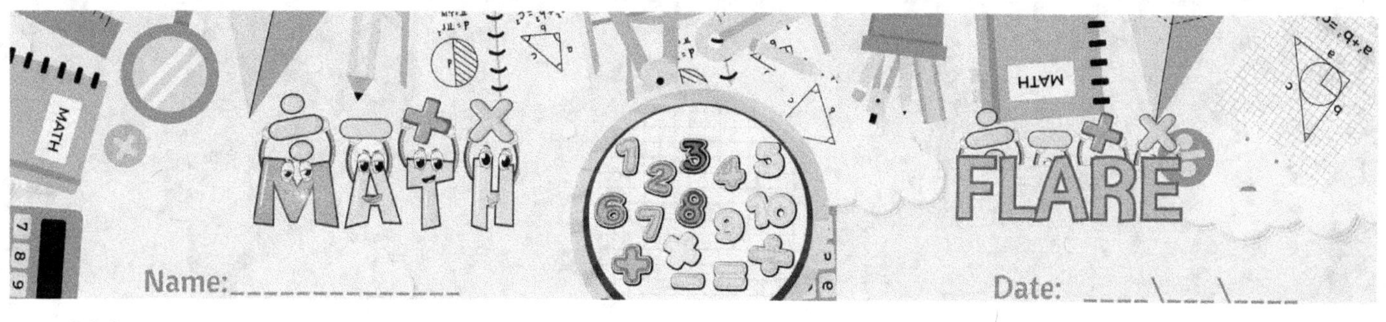

208. 11,000,000 = _______________________________

209. 5.3×10^7 = _______________________________

210. 2.286×10^7 = _______________________________

211. 4.768×10^7 = _______________________________

212. 2.1×10^7 = _______________________________

213. 8.64×10^7 = _______________________________

214. 9.9×10^7 = _______________________________

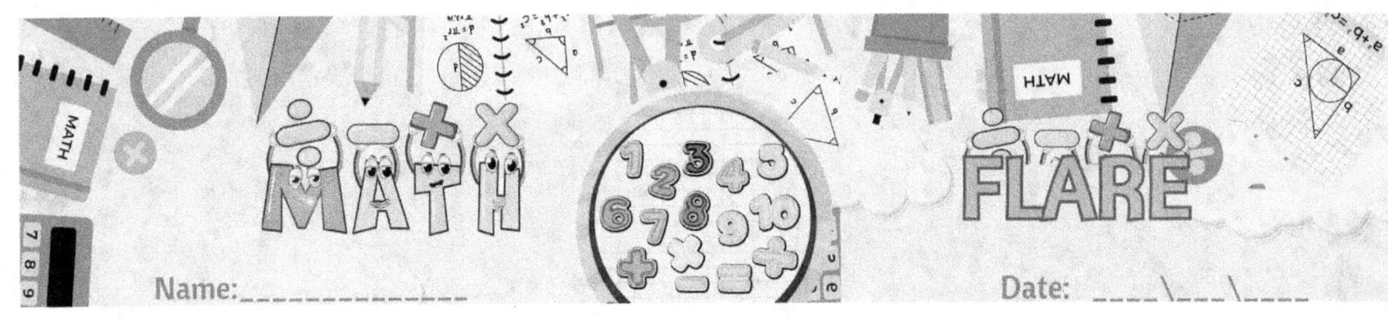

215. $81,570,000 =$ _______________________________

216. $30,000,000 =$ _______________________________

217. $59,000,000 =$ _______________________________

218. $89,550,000 =$ _______________________________

219. $67,580,000 =$ _______________________________

220. $40,000,000 =$ _______________________________

221. $3.3 \times 10^{7} =$ _______________________________

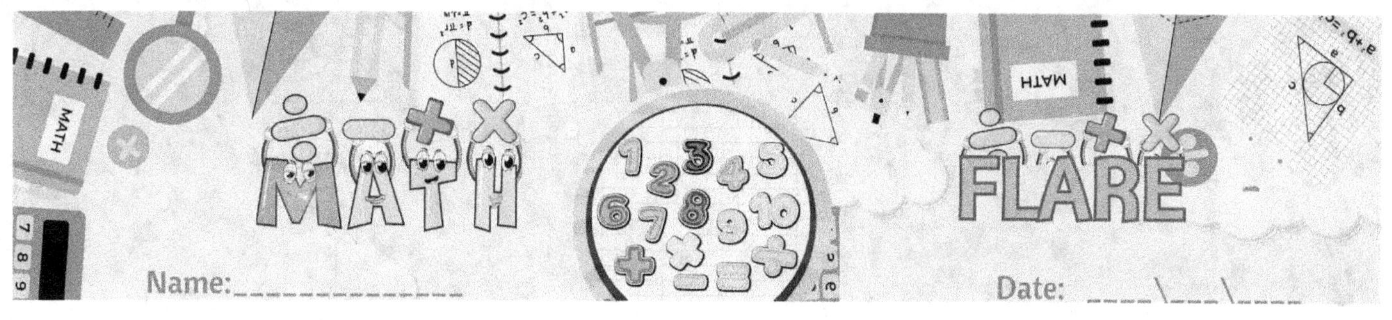

222. $80{,}200{,}000 =$ _______________

223. $22{,}200{,}000 =$ _______________

224. $8.3 \times 10^{7} =$ _______________

225. $93{,}530{,}000 =$ _______________

226. $3.68 \times 10^{7} =$ _______________

227. $65{,}000{,}000 =$ _______________

228. $7.54 \times 10^{7} =$ _______________

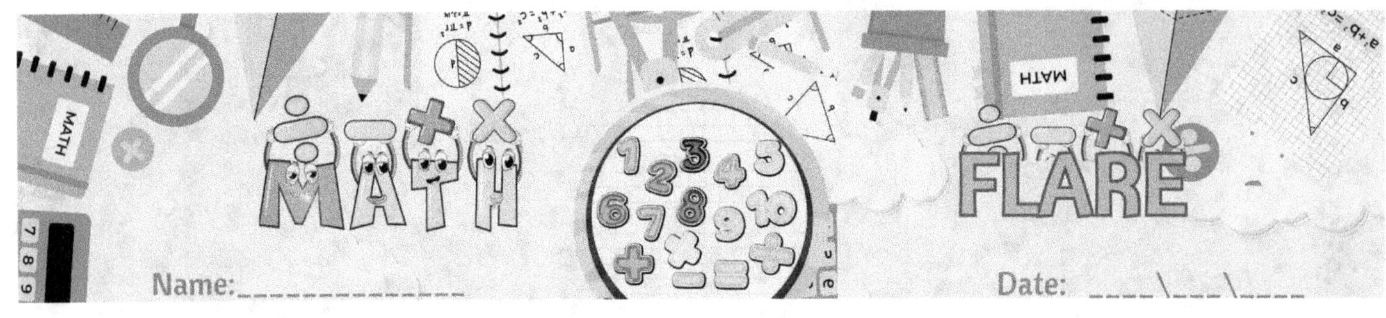

229. $29{,}000{,}000 =$ _______________________

230. $6 \times 10^{7} =$ _______________________

231. $6.81 \times 10^{7} =$ _______________________

232. $84{,}800{,}000 =$ _______________________

233. $89{,}600{,}000 =$ _______________________

234. $8.9 \times 10^{7} =$ _______________________

235. $1.832 \times 10^{7} =$ _______________________

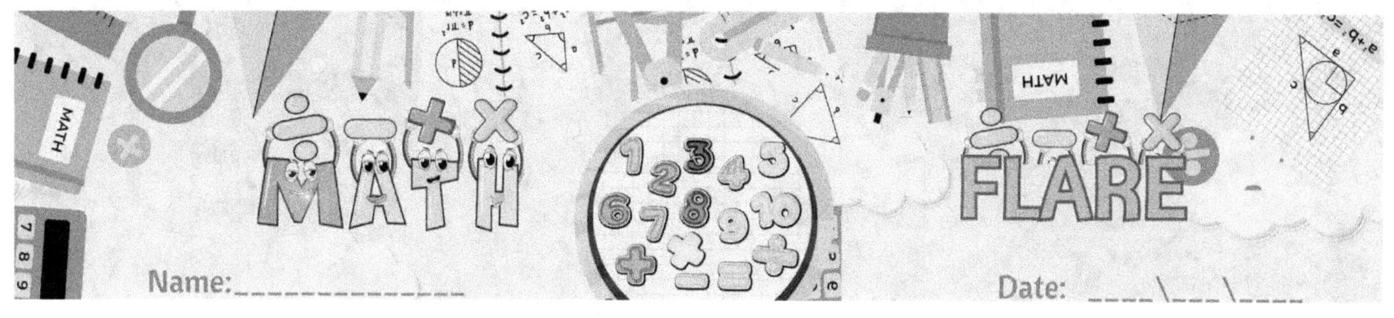

236. $41{,}200{,}000 =$ ______________________

237. $2.12 \times 10^{7} =$ ______________________

238. $3.337 \times 10^{7} =$ ______________________

239. $72{,}300{,}000 =$ ______________________

240. $48{,}400{,}000 =$ ______________________

241. $8.43 \times 10^{7} =$ ______________________

242. $4.5 \times 10^{7} =$ ______________________

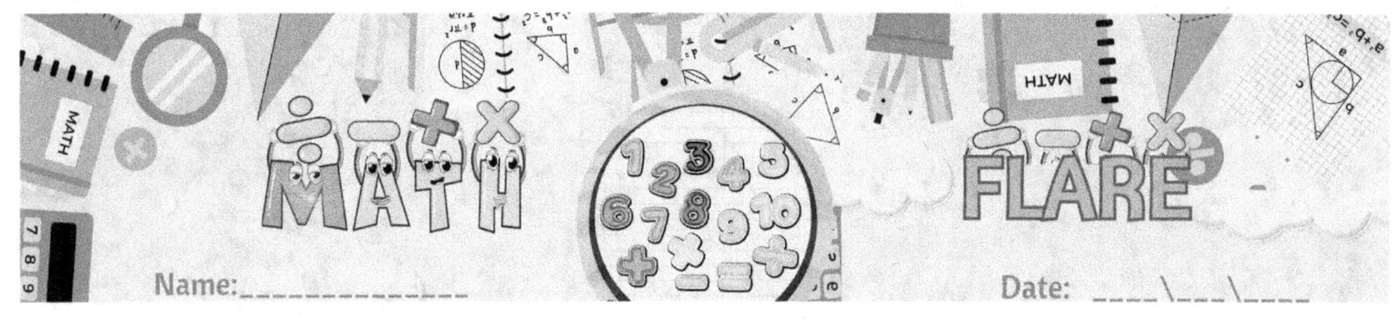

243. $63,400,000 =$ _______________

244. $23,620,000 =$ _______________

245. $42,900,000 =$ _______________

246. $9.474 \times 10^7 =$ _______________

247. $18,100,000 =$ _______________

248. $85,600,000 =$ _______________

249. $8.1 \times 10^7 =$ _______________

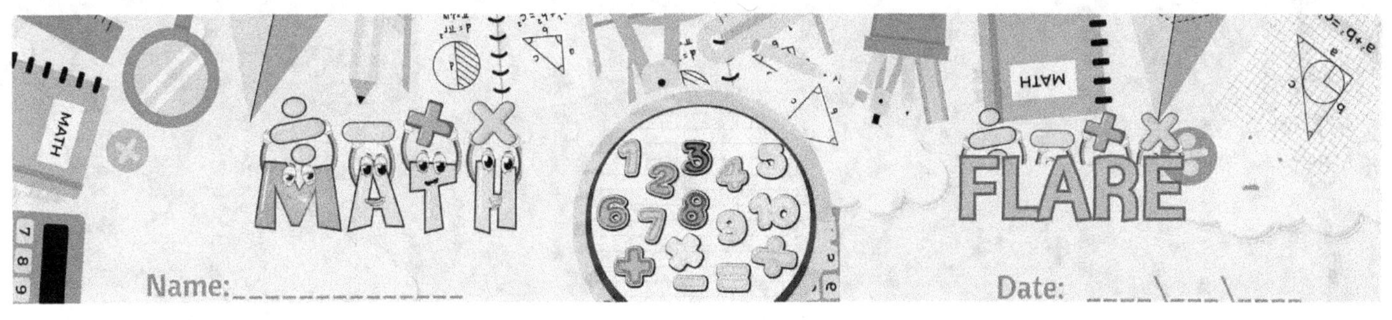

250. $9.3 \times 10^7 =$ _______________________________________

251. $3.7 \times 10^7 =$ _______________________________________

252. $7.108 \times 10^7 =$ _______________________________________

253. $2.7 \times 10^7 =$ _______________________________________

254. $12{,}800{,}000 =$ _______________________________________

255. $43{,}000{,}000 =$ _______________________________________

256. $1.13 \times 10^7 =$ _______________________________________

257. $11{,}490{,}000 =$ _______________________________

258. $7.39 \times 10^{7} =$ _______________________________

259. $47{,}000{,}000 =$ _______________________________

260. $2.516 \times 10^{7} =$ _______________________________

261. $60{,}990{,}000 =$ _______________________________

262. $61{,}690{,}000 =$ _______________________________

263. $26{,}690{,}000 =$ _______________________________

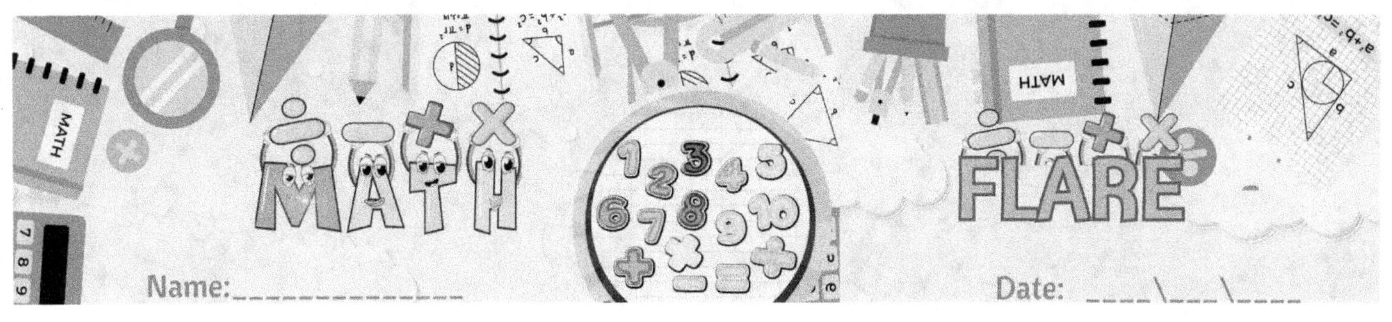

264. 4.8×10^{7} = _________________________

265. 9.44×10^{7} = _________________________

266. $94{,}160{,}000$ = _________________________

267. $18{,}160{,}000$ = _________________________

268. $28{,}000{,}000$ = _________________________

269. $44{,}800{,}000$ = _________________________

270. 7.917×10^{7} = _________________________

271. $9.104 \times 10^{7} =$ _______________________________

272. $97{,}830{,}000 =$ _______________________________

273. $3.99 \times 10^{7} =$ _______________________________

274. $96{,}930{,}000 =$ _______________________________

275. $22{,}400{,}000 =$ _______________________________

276. $30{,}480{,}000 =$ _______________________________

277. $55{,}600{,}000 =$ _______________________________

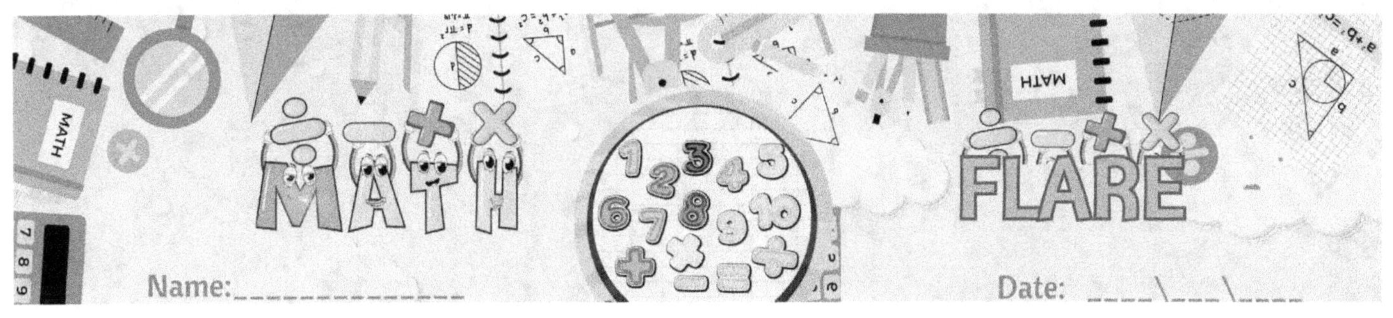

278. 23,000,000 = _______________________

279. 98,200,000 = _______________________

280. 41,000,000 = _______________________

281. 81,200,000 = _______________________

282. 5.09×10^7 = _______________________

283. 14,170,000 = _______________________

284. 1.17×10^7 = _______________________

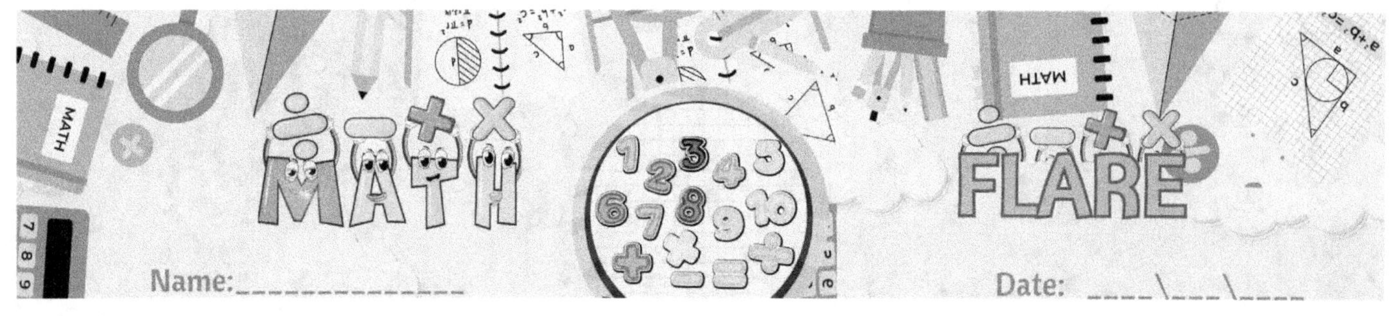

285. 25,000,000 = _______________________

286. 31,000,000 = _______________________

287. 68,000,000 = _______________________

288. 1.5×10^7 = _______________________

289. 67,260,000 = _______________________

290. 1.884×10^7 = _______________________

291. 7.255×10^7 = _______________________

292. $92{,}000{,}000 =$ ___________

293. $7.789 \times 10^{7} =$ ___________

294. $4.83 \times 10^{7} =$ ___________

295. $21{,}110{,}000 =$ ___________

296. $71{,}430{,}000 =$ ___________

297. $8.839 \times 10^{7} =$ ___________

298. $57{,}080{,}000 =$ ___________

299. 71,800,000 = _______________________

300. 4.695×10^7 = _______________________

301. 17,000,000 = _______________________

302. 7×10^7 = _______________________

303. 66,000,000 = _______________________

304. 44,600,000 = _______________________

305. 47,200,000 = _______________________

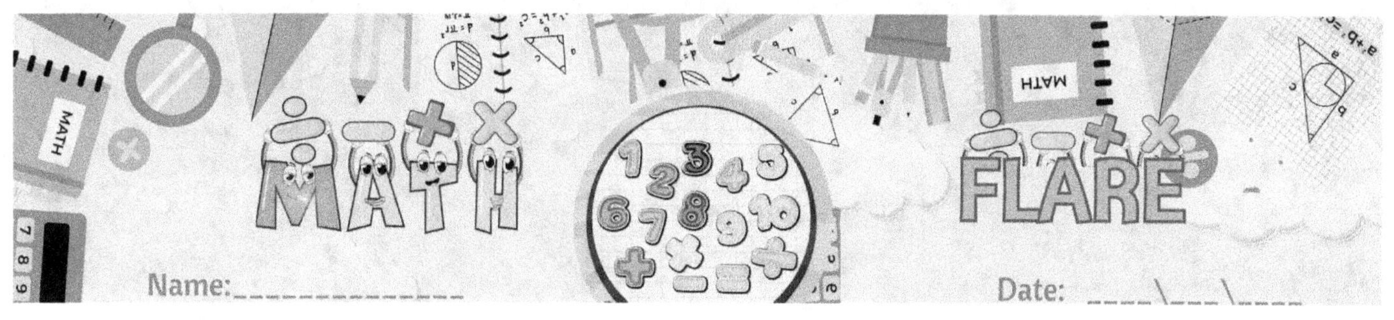

306. 84,900,000 = _______________

307. 2.361×10^{7} = _______________

308. 3.02×10^{7} = _______________

309. 36,000,000 = _______________

310. 85,000,000 = _______________

311. 1×10^{7} = _______________

312. 91,000,000 = _______________

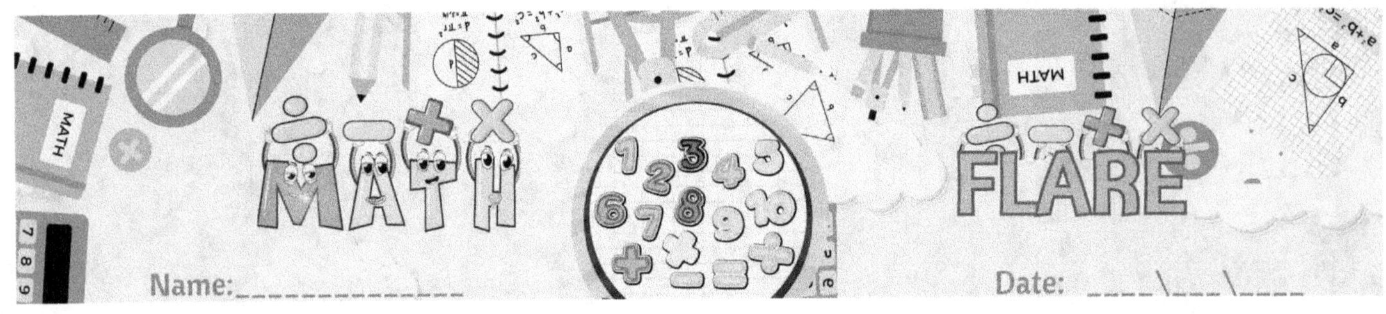

313. 14,000,000 = _______________________________

314. 44,000,000 = _______________________________

315. 98,700,000 = _______________________________

316. 74,000,000 = _______________________________

317. 39,330,000 = _______________________________

318. 5.59×10^{7} = _______________________________

319. 5.6×10^{7} = _______________________________

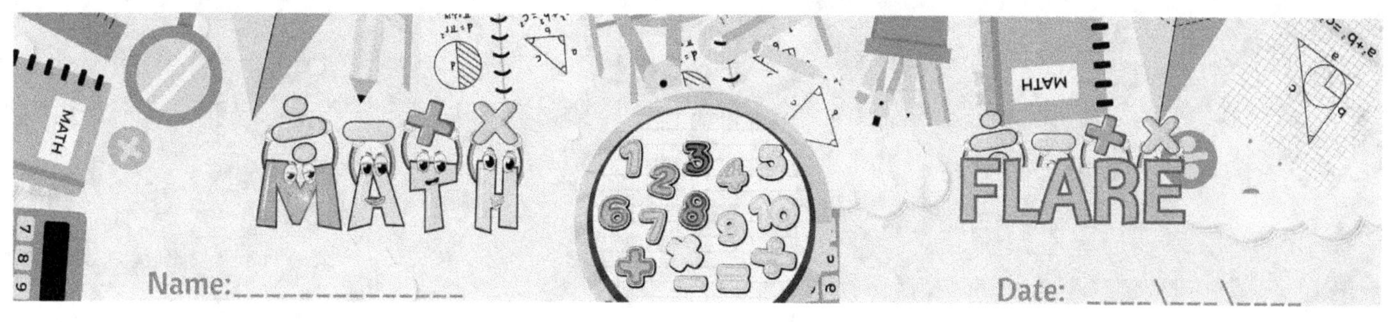

320. 7.7×10^{7} = ___________

321. $64{,}000{,}000$ = ___________

322. 1.578×10^{7} = ___________

323. 4.041×10^{7} = ___________

324. $73{,}000{,}000$ = ___________

325. 6.983×10^{7} = ___________

326. $87{,}500{,}000$ = ___________

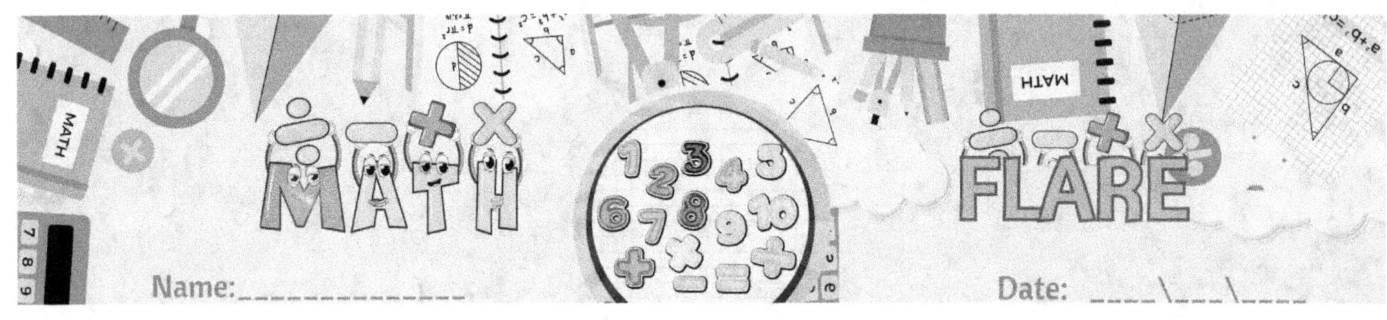

327. $8.53 \times 10^{7} =$ ______________________

328. $49{,}000{,}000 =$ ______________________

329. $71{,}170{,}000 =$ ______________________

330. $8.524 \times 10^{7} =$ ______________________

331. $21{,}880{,}000 =$ ______________________

332. $6.3 \times 10^{7} =$ ______________________

333. $66{,}050{,}000 =$ ______________________

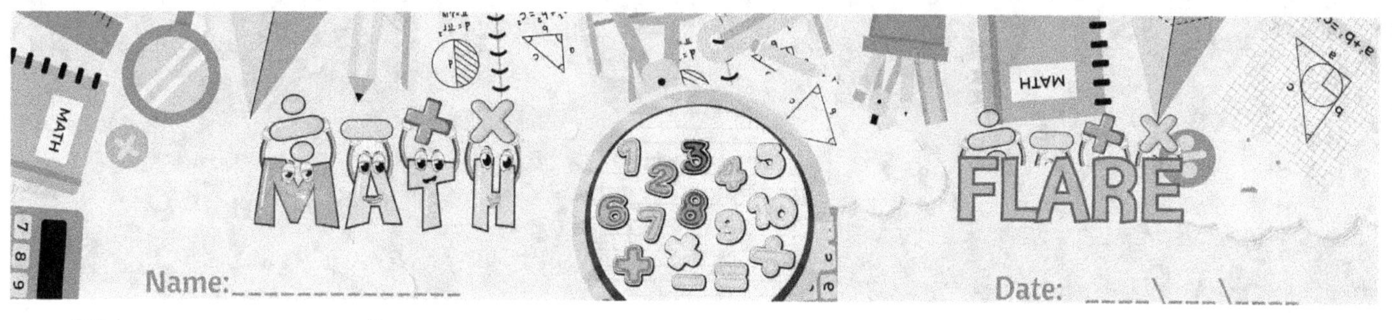

334. $3.492 \times 10^{7} =$ _______________________

335. $3.5 \times 10^{7} =$ _______________________

336. $69,600,000 =$ _______________________

337. $7.055 \times 10^{7} =$ _______________________

338. $76,900,000 =$ _______________________

339. $3.902 \times 10^{7} =$ _______________________

340. $5.5 \times 10^{7} =$ _______________________

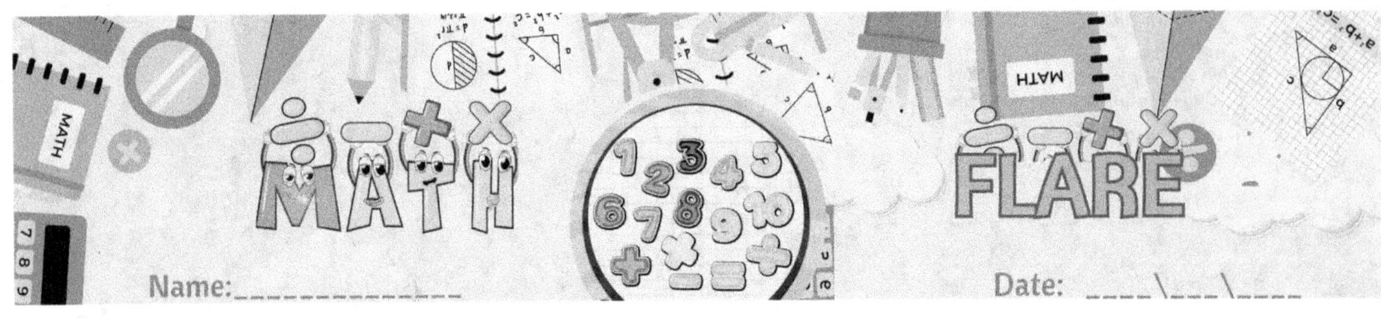

341. 92,120,000 = _______________________________

342. 2.68×10^7 = _______________________________

343. 9.17×10^7 = _______________________________

344. 46,800,000 = _______________________________

345. 9.7×10^7 = _______________________________

346. 8.317×10^7 = _______________________________

347. 4.979×10^7 = _______________________________

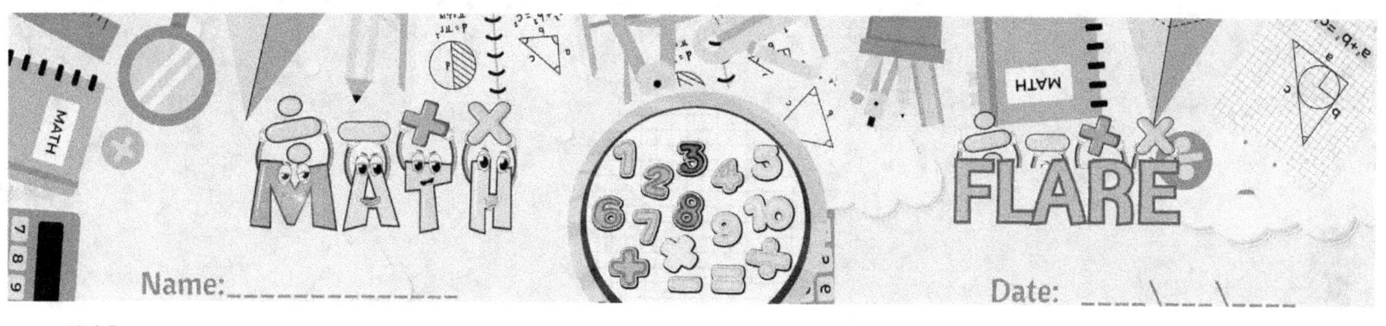

348. $65,660,000 =$ _________________

349. $9.91 \times 10^{7} =$ _________________

350. $8.622 \times 10^{7} =$ _________________

351. $11,820,000 =$ _________________

352. $4.814 \times 10^{7} =$ _________________

353. $64,600,000 =$ _________________

354. $33,620,000 =$ _________________

355. $7.05 \times 10^7 =$ _______________________

356. $8.81 \times 10^7 =$ _______________________

357. $20{,}030{,}000 =$ _______________________

358. $8.23 \times 10^7 =$ _______________________

359. $80{,}000{,}000 =$ _______________________

360. $8.01 \times 10^7 =$ _______________________

361. $6.42 \times 10^7 =$ _______________________

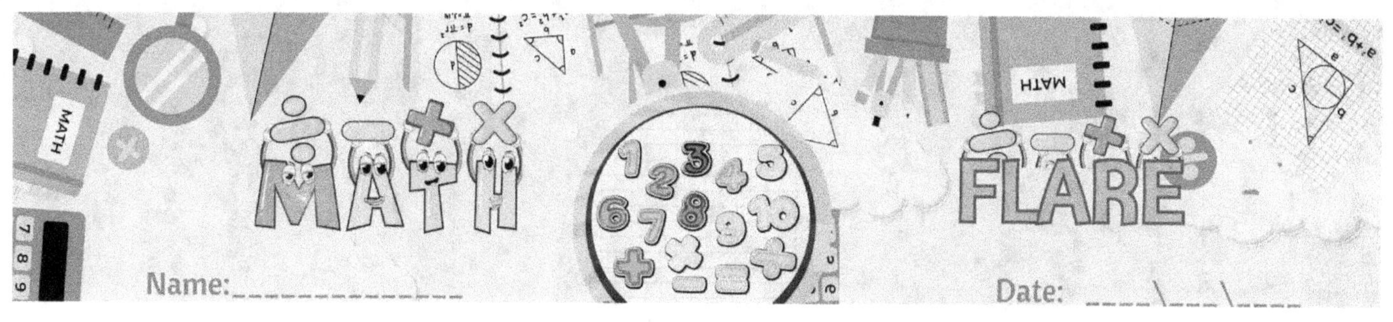

Name:_______________

Date: _______________

362. $7.9 \times 10^{7} =$ _______________________________

363. $1.634 \times 10^{7} =$ _______________________________

364. $75,510,000 =$ _______________________________

365. $7.1 \times 10^{7} =$ _______________________________

366. $5.481 \times 10^{7} =$ _______________________________

367. $8.26 \times 10^{7} =$ _______________________________

368. $4.522 \times 10^{7} =$ _______________________________

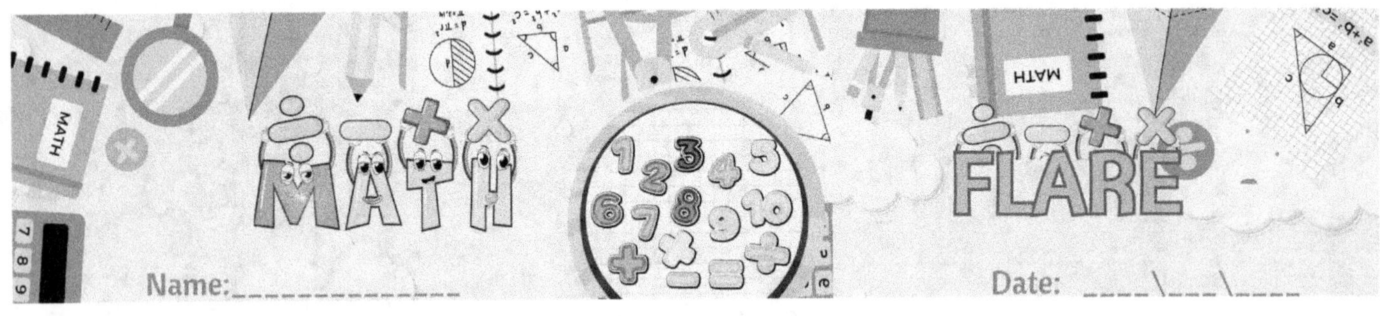

369. 95,000,000 = __________________________________

370. 8.8×10^{7} = __________________________________

371. 51,000,000 = __________________________________

372. 86,130,000 = __________________________________

373. 72,000,000 = __________________________________

374. 54,870,000 = __________________________________

375. 2.63×10^{7} = __________________________________

376. 53,480,000 = _______________________________

377. 6.2×10^{7} = _______________________________

378. 81,770,000 = _______________________________

379. 63,710,000 = _______________________________

380. 1.8×10^{7} = _______________________________

381. 2.826×10^{7} = _______________________________

382. 43,860,000 = _______________________________

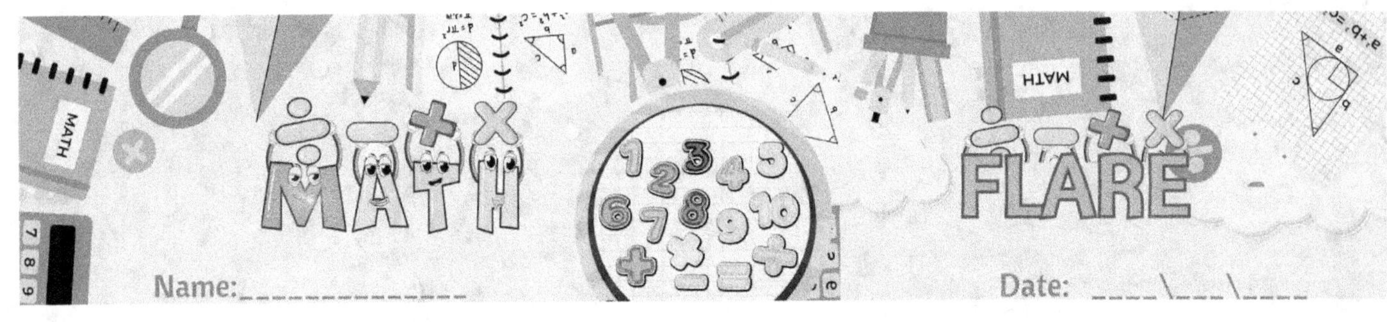

383. $5.436 \times 10^{7} =$ _________________________

384. $19{,}150{,}000 =$ _________________________

385. $9.04 \times 10^{7} =$ _________________________

386. $3.659 \times 10^{7} =$ _________________________

387. $5.513 \times 10^{7} =$ _________________________

388. $27{,}620{,}000 =$ _________________________

389. $1.959 \times 10^{7} =$ _________________________

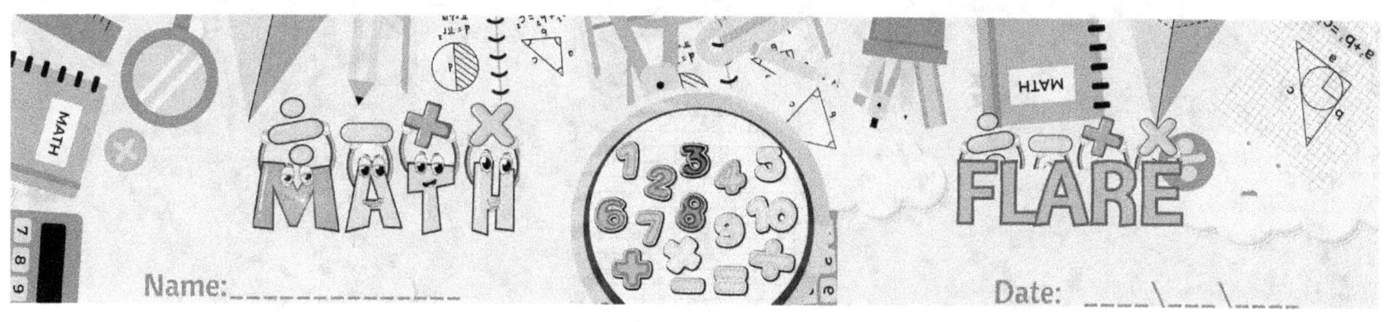

390. $84{,}000{,}000 = $ ______________________

391. $39{,}440{,}000 = $ ______________________

392. $4.11 \times 10^{7} = $ ______________________

393. $6.209 \times 10^{7} = $ ______________________

394. $7.09 \times 10^{7} = $ ______________________

395. $41{,}650{,}000 = $ ______________________

396. $6.41 \times 10^{7} = $ ______________________

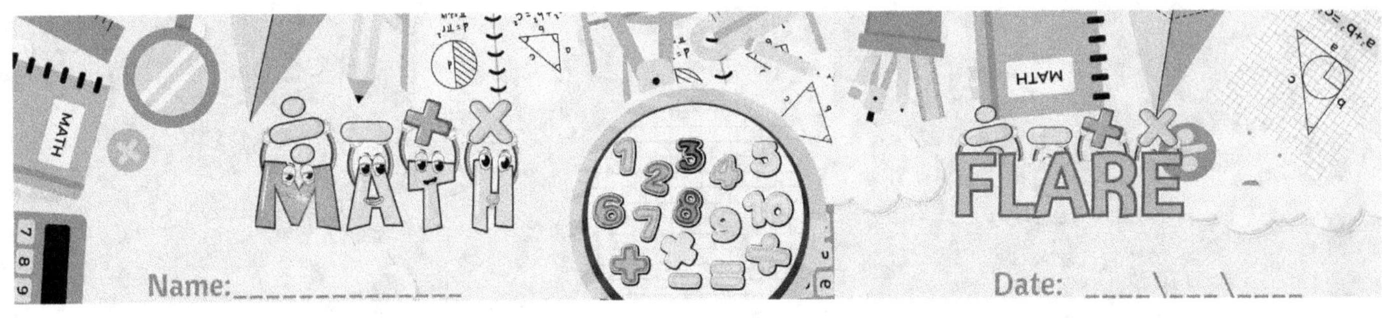

397. 12,000,000 = _______________________________

398. 83,530,000 = _______________________________

399. 51,220,000 = _______________________________

400. 49,530,000 = _______________________________

401. 2.85×10^{7} = _______________________________

402. 4.28×10^{7} = _______________________________

403. 37,800,000 = _______________________________

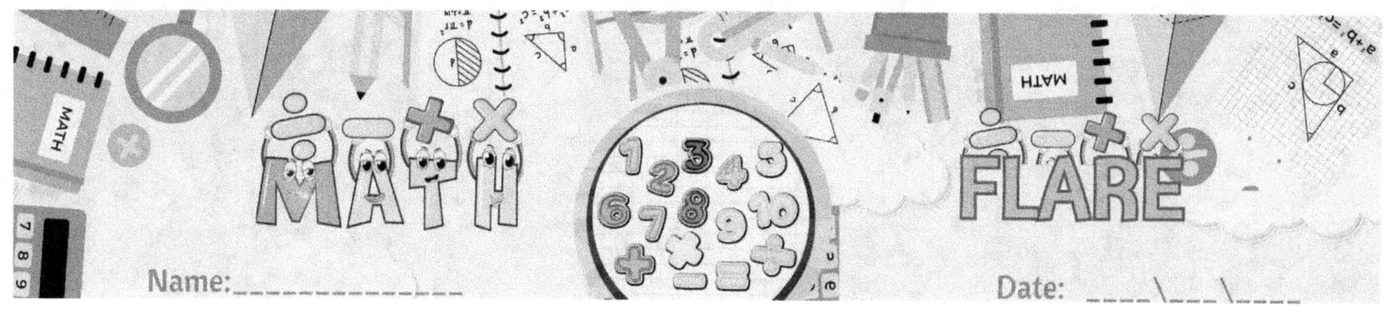

404. 16,650,000 = _______________________________

405. 62,000,000 = _______________________________

406. 4.4×10^{7} = _______________________________

407. 27,500,000 = _______________________________

408. 12,800,000 = _______________________________

409. 4.167×10^{7} = _______________________________

410. 5.6×10^{7} = _______________________________

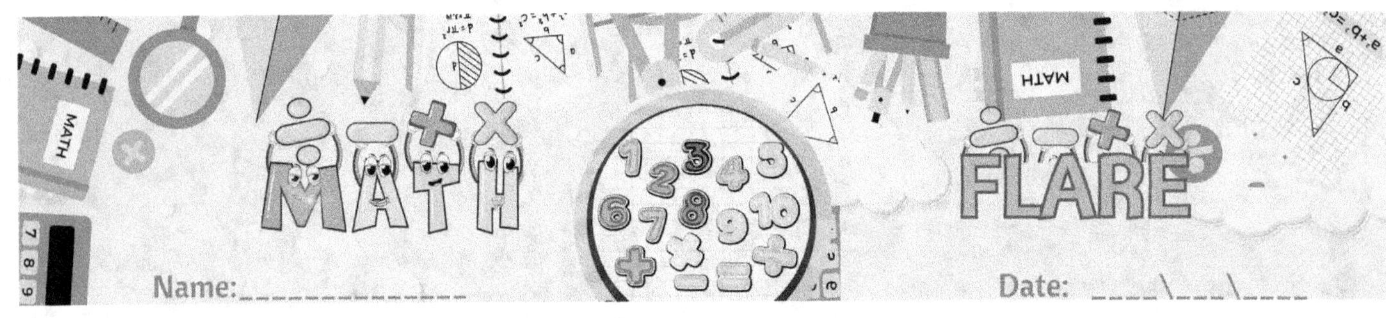

411. 18,260,000 = _______________________________

412. 2.51×10^7 = _______________________________

413. 99,940,000 = _______________________________

414. 3.033×10^7 = _______________________________

415. 7.383×10^7 = _______________________________

416. 74,000,000 = _______________________________

417. 8.4×10^7 = _______________________________

418. $5.8 \times 10^7 =$ ______________________

419. $76{,}000{,}000 =$ ______________________

420. $1.9 \times 10^7 =$ ______________________

421. $4.294 \times 10^7 =$ ______________________

422. $40{,}640{,}000 =$ ______________________

423. $74{,}900{,}000 =$ ______________________

424. $8.04 \times 10^7 =$ ______________________

425. 26,830,000 = _______________________________

426. 3×10^{7} = _______________________________

427. 33,400,000 = _______________________________

428. 8.702×10^{7} = _______________________________

429. 9.03×10^{7} = _______________________________

430. 1.42×10^{7} = _______________________________

431. 84,110,000 = _______________________________

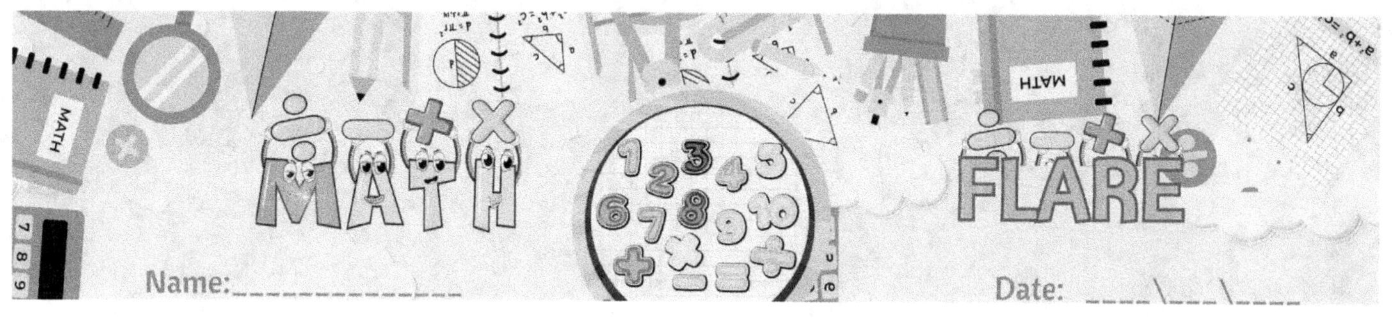

432. $4.627 \times 10^7 =$ ______________________

433. $52{,}900{,}000 =$ ______________________

434. $45{,}780{,}000 =$ ______________________

435. $1.1 \times 10^7 =$ ______________________

436. $87{,}000{,}000 =$ ______________________

437. $5.16 \times 10^7 =$ ______________________

438. $33{,}650{,}000 =$ ______________________

439. 99,100,000 = _______________________________

440. 24,300,000 = _______________________________

441. 2.57×10^7 = _______________________________

442. 6.442×10^7 = _______________________________

443. 24,620,000 = _______________________________

444. 8.516×10^7 = _______________________________

445. 1.228×10^7 = _______________________________

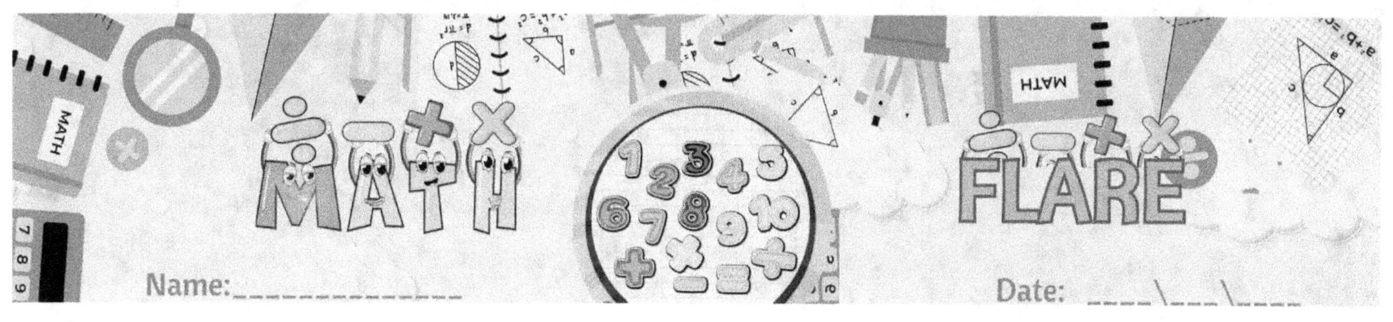

446. $4.075 \times 10^{7} = $ _______________________

447. $49{,}000{,}000 = $ _______________________

448. $45{,}300{,}000 = $ _______________________

449. $4.33 \times 10^{7} = $ _______________________

450. $5.97 \times 10^{7} = $ _______________________

451. $40{,}000{,}000 = $ _______________________

452. $6.71 \times 10^{7} = $ _______________________

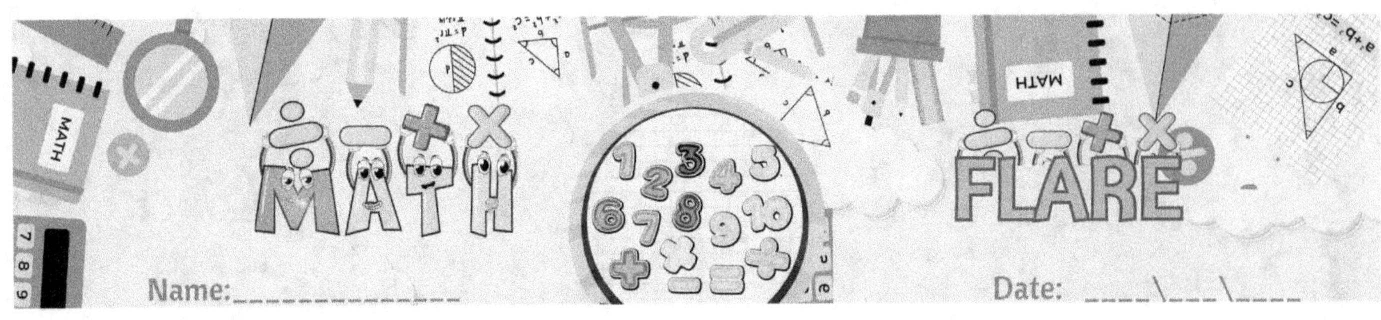

453. $2.92 \times 10^7 =$ _______________________

454. $24{,}900{,}000 =$ _______________________

455. $9 \times 10^7 =$ _______________________

456. $74{,}800{,}000 =$ _______________________

457. $5.216 \times 10^7 =$ _______________________

458. $29{,}910{,}000 =$ _______________________

459. $1.4 \times 10^7 =$ _______________________

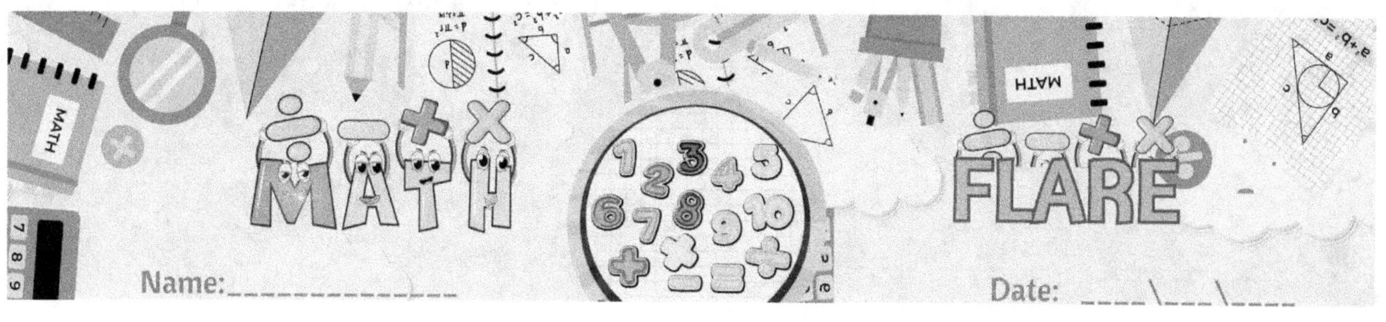

460. 48,300,000 = _______________________________

461. 7.8×10^7 = _______________________________

462. 1.294×10^7 = _______________________________

463. 4.017×10^7 = _______________________________

464. 5.9×10^7 = _______________________________

465. 67,000,000 = _______________________________

466. 25,200,000 = _______________________________

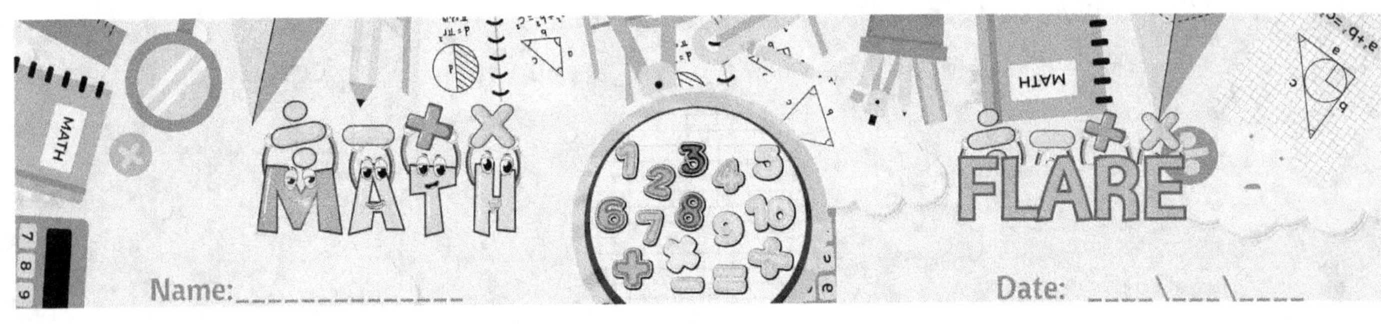

467. 16,960,000 = ________________________________

468. 7.09×10^{7} = ________________________________

469. 55,000,000 = ________________________________

470. 3.04×10^{7} = ________________________________

471. 72,250,000 = ________________________________

472. 27,400,000 = ________________________________

473. 3.903×10^{7} = ________________________________

474. $4.05 \times 10^7 =$ _______________________

475. $3.223 \times 10^7 =$ _______________________

476. $1.6 \times 10^7 =$ _______________________

477. $21,770,000 =$ _______________________

478. $16,800,000 =$ _______________________

479. $64,000,000 =$ _______________________

480. $84,600,000 =$ _______________________

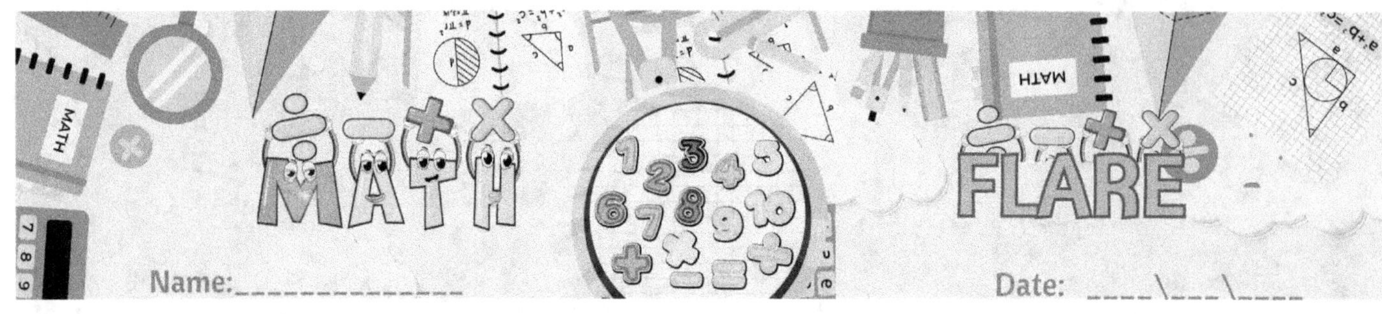

481. 27,000,000 = _______________________________

482. 3.219×10^7 = _______________________________

483. 3.33×10^7 = _______________________________

484. 4.073×10^7 = _______________________________

485. 7.992×10^7 = _______________________________

486. 8.39×10^7 = _______________________________

487. 20,700,000 = _______________________________

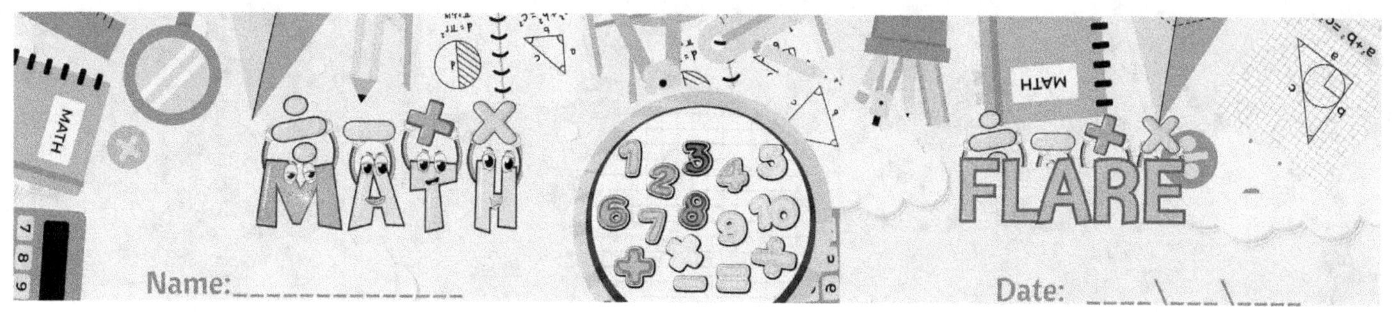

488. $8.9 \times 10^{7} =$ _________________________

489. $4.74 \times 10^{7} =$ _________________________

490. $37,600,000 =$ _________________________

491. $96,500,000 =$ _________________________

492. $9.7 \times 10^{7} =$ _________________________

493. $83,000,000 =$ _________________________

494. $1.357 \times 10^{7} =$ _________________________

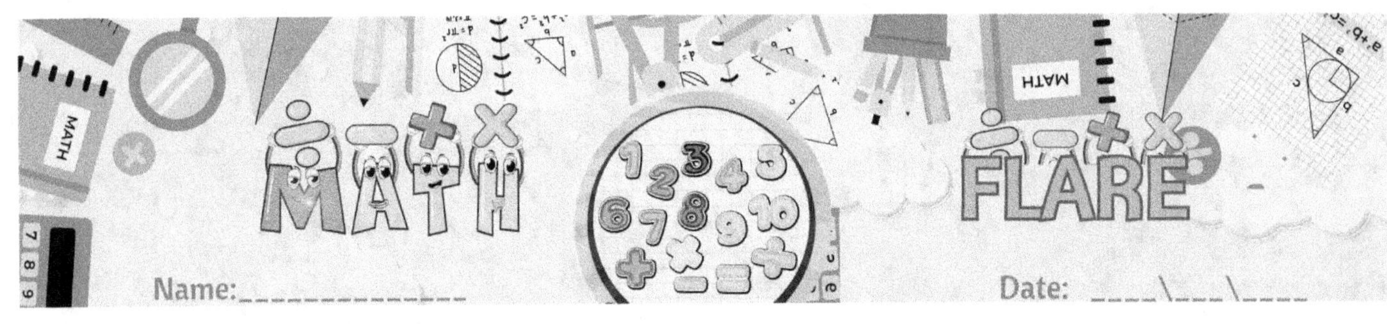

495. $7.635 \times 10^{7} =$ _______________________

496. $2.4 \times 10^{7} =$ _______________________

497. $39,730,000 =$ _______________________

498. $29,970,000 =$ _______________________

499. $48,340,000 =$ _______________________

500. $10,600,000 =$ _______________________

ANSWERS

Page 1: Exponents

1. 83,521	2. 1,419,857	3. 8	4. 2,401
5. 1/65536	6. 1	7. 121	8. 1/3375
9. 1/225	10. 3,125	11. 10	12. 1/7776
13. 27	14. 169	15. 20	16. 100
17. 1	18. 1	19. 1/7	20. 248,832
21. 1/243	22. 20,736	23. 1,048,576	24. 1/64
25. 4,913	26. 289	27. 1/3	28. 65,536
29. 10,000	30. 1/18	31. 1/16807	32. 216
33. 64	34. 1/14	35. 6	36. 1/32
37. 1/6859	38. 12	39. 1	40. 2,197
41. 36	42. 1/5	43. 1/20736	44. 1/256
45. 1/50625	46. 1/104976	47. 3,200,000	48. 196
49. 1/2476099	50. 1/1296	51. 5	52. 1/216
53. 1/4	54. 1/14641	55. 1/10000	56. 13
57. 400	58. 16	59. 1	60. 4
61. 9	62. 1,000	63. 759,375	64. 1/10
65. 1/2401	66. 1/16	67. 1/3200000	68. 371,293
69. 1/36	70. 1/1419857	71. 1/15	72. 256
73. 1	74. 1	75. 59,049	76. 5,832

77. 14,641	78. 1	79. 100,000	80. 625
81. 16,807	82. 160,000	83. 1/38416	84. 1
85. 25	86. 1/64	87. 3	88. 16
89. 7	90. 81	91. 1	92. 1
93. 1/32768	94. 11	95. 243	96. 1/5832
97. 1,331	98. 1/8	99. 1/1889568	100. 4,096
101. 17	102. 1/1728	103. 4	104. 1/6
105. 1/160000	106. 1/537824	107. 1/28561	108. 1,889,568
109. 1/100000	110. 3,375	111. 1/27	112. 1/2
113. 161,051	114. 1	115. 64	116. 1
117. 1/6561	118. 1/20	119. 18	120. 1/400
121. 1/4	122. 1/1024	123. 1/17	124. 1
125. 2,476,099	126. 6,561	127. 32	128. 125
129. 38,416	130. 1	131. 1/512	132. 1/361
133. 1	134. 1/161051	135. 32,768	136. 9
137. 1/12	138. 81	139. 1/16	140. 1/371293
141. 6,859	142. 1	143. 8,000	144. 1/83521
145. 1/16	146. 1/1048576	147. 1/59049	148. 1/130321
149. 1/4913	150. 1,024	151. 1/81	152. 8
153. 15	154. 1/169	155. 7,776	156. 130,321
157. 1/100	158. 1	159. 28,561	160. 1

161. 324

162. 537,824

163. 1

164. 225

165. 1/729

166. 1/324

167. 14

168. 16

169. 1/4096

170. 50,625

171. 1/248832

172. 1/9

173. 1/8000

174. 49

175. 729

176. 144

177. 1,728

178. 1,296

179. 512

180. 1

181. 1/2197

182. 1

183. 1/3125

184. 343

185. 361

186. 104,976

187. 1/625

188. 1

189. 1

190. 1/144

191. 1/759375

192. 4,096

193. 2,744

194. 1/4096

195. 1/2744

196. 1/81

197. 1

198. 1/343

199. 1/289

200. 1/13

Page 18: Scientific Notation

201. 6.1×10^7

202. 43,500,000

203. 8.964×10^7

204. 7.471×10^7

205. 3.092×10^7

206. 6.9×10^7

207. 6.73×10^7

208. 1.1×10^7

209. 53,000,000

210. 22,860,000

211. 47,680,000

212. 21,000,000

213. 86,400,000

214. 99,000,000

215. 8.157×10^7

216. 3×10^7

217. 5.9×10^7

218. 8.955×10^7

219. 6.758×10^7

220. 4×10^7

221. 33,000,000

222. 8.02×10^7

223. 2.22×10^7

224. 83,000,000

225. 9.353×10^7

226. 36,800,000

227. 6.5×10^7

228. 75,400,000

229. 2.9×10^7

230. 60,000,000

231. 68,100,000

232. 8.48×10^7

233. 8.96×10^7

234. 89,000,000

235. 18,320,000

236. 4.12×10^7

237. 21,200,000

238. 33,370,000

239. 7.23×10^7

240. 4.84×10^7

241. 84,300,000

242. 45,000,000

243. 6.34×10^7

244. 2.362×10^7

245. 4.29×10^7

246. 94,740,000

247. 1.81×10^7

248. 8.56×10^7

249. 81,000,000

250. 93,000,000

251. 37,000,000

252. 71,080,000

253. 27,000,000

254. 1.28×10^7

255. 4.3×10^7

256. 11,300,000

257. 1.149×10^7

258. 73,900,000

259. 4.7×10^7

260. 25,160,000

261. 6.099×10^7

262. 6.169×10^7

263. 2.669×10^7

264. 48,000,000

265. 94,400,000

266. 9.416×10^7

267. 1.816×10^7

268. 2.8×10^7

269. 4.48×10^7

270. 79,170,000

271. 91,040,000

272. 9.783×10^7

273. 39,900,000

274. 9.693×10^7

275. 2.24×10^7

276. 3.048×10^7

277. 5.56×10^7

278. 2.3×10^7

279. 9.82×10^7

280. 4.1×10^7

281. 8.12×10^7

282. 50,900,000

283. 1.417×10^7

284. 11,700,000

285. 2.5×10^7

286. 3.1×10^7

287. 6.8×10^7

288. 15,000,000

289. 6.726×10^7

290. 18,840,000

291. 72,550,000

292. 9.2×10^7

293. 77,890,000

294. 48,300,000   295. 2.111 × 10^7   296. 7.143 × 10^7

297. 88,390,000   298. 5.708 × 10^7   299. 7.18 × 10^7

300. 46,950,000   301. 1.7 × 10^7   302. 70,000,000

303. 6.6 × 10^7   304. 4.46 × 10^7   305. 4.72 × 10^7

306. 8.49 × 10^7   307. 23,610,000   308. 30,200,000

309. 3.6 × 10^7   310. 8.5 × 10^7   311. 10,000,000

312. 9.1 × 10^7   313. 1.4 × 10^7   314. 4.4 × 10^7

315. 9.87 × 10^7   316. 7.4 × 10^7   317. 3.933 × 10^7

318. 55,900,000   319. 56,000,000   320. 77,000,000

321. 6.4 × 10^7   322. 15,780,000   323. 40,410,000

324. 7.3 × 10^7   325. 69,830,000   326. 8.75 × 10^7

327. 85,300,000   328. 4.9 × 10^7   329. 7.117 × 10^7

330. 85,240,000   331. 2.188 × 10^7   332. 63,000,000

333. 6.605 × 10^7   334. 34,920,000   335. 35,000,000

336. 6.96 × 10^7   337. 70,550,000   338. 7.69 × 10^7

339. 39,020,000   340. 55,000,000   341. 9.212 × 10^7

342. 26,800,000   343. 91,700,000   344. 4.68 × 10^7

345. 97,000,000   346. 83,170,000   347. 49,790,000

348. 6.566 × 10^7   349. 99,100,000   350. 86,220,000

351. 1.182 × 10^7   352. 48,140,000   353. 6.46 × 10^7

354. 3.362 × 10^7   355. 70,500,000   356. 88,100,000

357. 2.003×10^7

358. 82,300,000

359. 8×10^7

360. 80,100,000

361. 64,200,000

362. 79,000,000

363. 16,340,000

364. 7.551×10^7

365. 71,000,000

366. 54,810,000

367. 82,600,000

368. 45,220,000

369. 9.5×10^7

370. 88,000,000

371. 5.1×10^7

372. 8.613×10^7

373. 7.2×10^7

374. 5.487×10^7

375. 26,300,000

376. 5.348×10^7

377. 62,000,000

378. 8.177×10^7

379. 6.371×10^7

380. 18,000,000

381. 28,260,000

382. 4.386×10^7

383. 54,360,000

384. 1.915×10^7

385. 90,400,000

386. 36,590,000

387. 55,130,000

388. 2.762×10^7

389. 19,590,000

390. 8.4×10^7

391. 3.944×10^7

392. 41,100,000

393. 62,090,000

394. 70,900,000

395. 4.165×10^7

396. 64,100,000

397. 1.2×10^7

398. 8.353×10^7

399. 5.122×10^7

400. 4.953×10^7

Page 46: Scientific Notation

401. 28,500,000

402. 42,800,000

403. 3.78×10^7

404. 1.665×10^7

405. 6.2×10^7

406. 44,000,000

407. 2.75×10^7

408. 1.28×10^7

409. 41,670,000

410. 56,000,000

411. 1.826×10^7

412. 25,100,000

413. 9.994×10^7

414. 30,330,000

415. 73,830,000

416. 7.4 × 10^7   417. 84,000,000   418. 58,000,000

419. 7.6 × 10^7   420. 19,000,000   421. 42,940,000

422. 4.064 × 10^7   423. 7.49 × 10^7   424. 80,400,000

425. 2.683 × 10^7   426. 30,000,000   427. 3.34 × 10^7

428. 87,020,000   429. 90,300,000   430. 14,200,000

431. 8.411 × 10^7   432. 46,270,000   433. 5.29 × 10^7

434. 4.578 × 10^7   435. 11,000,000   436. 8.7 × 10^7

437. 51,600,000   438. 3.365 × 10^7   439. 9.91 × 10^7

440. 2.43 × 10^7   441. 25,700,000   442. 64,420,000

443. 2.462 × 10^7   444. 85,160,000   445. 12,280,000

446. 40,750,000   447. 4.9 × 10^7   448. 4.53 × 10^7

449. 43,300,000   450. 59,700,000   451. 4 × 10^7

452. 67,100,000   453. 29,200,000   454. 2.49 × 10^7

455. 90,000,000   456. 7.48 × 10^7   457. 52,160,000

458. 2.991 × 10^7   459. 14,000,000   460. 4.83 × 10^7

461. 78,000,000   462. 12,940,000   463. 40,170,000

464. 59,000,000   465. 6.7 × 10^7   466. 2.52 × 10^7

467. 1.696 × 10^7   468. 70,900,000   469. 5.5 × 10^7

470. 30,400,000   471. 7.225 × 10^7   472. 2.74 × 10^7

473. 39,030,000   474. 40,500,000   475. 32,230,000

476. 16,000,000   477. 2.177 × 10^7   478. 1.68 × 10^7

479. 6.4×10^7

480. 8.46×10^7

481. 2.7×10^7

482. 32,190,000

483. 33,300,000

484. 40,730,000

485. 79,920,000

486. 83,900,000

487. 2.07×10^7

488. 89,000,000

489. 47,400,000

490. 3.76×10^7

491. 9.65×10^7

492. 97,000,000

493. 8.3×10^7

494. 13,570,000

495. 76,350,000

496. 24,000,000

497. 3.973×10^7

498. 2.997×10^7

499. 4.834×10^7

500. 1.06×10^7